Die drei ???®
Vampire City

von Marco Sonnleitner

PONS GmbH
Stuttgart

PONS

Die drei ???®

Vampire City

von Marco Sonnleitner
Englisch von Marion Charles

basierend auf „Die drei ??? - Stadt der Vampire" von Marco Sonnleitner

Die drei ??? – Stadt der Vampire © 2008 Franckh-Kosmos
Verlags-GmbH & Co. KG, Stuttgart
Mit freundlicher Genehmigung der Universität von Michigan.
Based on characters by Robert Arthur.

Auflage A1 5 4 3 2 1 / 2012 2011 2010 2009

© PONS GmbH, Rotebühlstraße 77, 70178 Stuttgart, 2009
Produktinfos und Online-Shop: www.pons.de
E-Mail: info@pons.de
Online-Wörterbuch und Online-Bildwörterbuch: www.pons.eu
Alle Rechte vorbehalten.

Übersetzung: Marion Charles
Annotationen und Übungen: Anneli Jefferson
Redaktion: Angelique Slaats
Logoentwurf: Erwin Poell, Heidelberg
Logoüberarbeitung: Sabine Redlin, Ludwigsburg
Titelillustration: Silvia Christoph, Berlin
Einbandgestaltung: Daniel Müller, Stuttgart
Tonaufnahmen/Digital Mastering: allegria Musik-/Audioproduktion GbR
Sprecher: Brian Munatones
Layout/Satz: Satz und mehr, Besigheim
Druck und Bindung: L.E.G.O. S.p.A., Lavis (TN)

Printed in Italy.
ISBN: 978-3-12-010042-3

Inhaltsverzeichnis

Track	Inhalt	Seite
	Inhaltsangabe	5
	Auftretende Personen	7
01	1. The Ghost Town	9
02	2. Dark Memory	13
03	3. The Secret of Yonderwood	18
04	4. Seas of Blood	23
05	5. The Vampire Hunters	27
06	6. Ten little Indians	30
07	7. And Then There Were Only Nine	35
08	8. Once Bitten, Twice Shy!	40
09	9. Beyond the Woods	45
10	10. Night of Horror	49
11	11. The Year of Revenge	53
12	12. Searching for Clues	60
13	13. The Vampire's Crypt	65
14	14. No Time!	70
15	15. The Cat's Treasure	74
16	16. Experiments	78
17	17. The Real Scoundrel	83

Englisch-Deutsche Wortliste 89

Nützliche Detektiv-Ausdrücke 103

Übungen 105

Lösungen 118

Inhaltsangabe

Eine riesige Fledermaus versetzt die Kleinstadt Yonderwood in Angst und Schrecken. Der Großteil der Einwohner hat bereits das Weite gesucht, nachdem einige Menschen mit Bissspuren und einer Menge Blut in ihren Betten erwacht sind. Justus, Peter und Bob haben noch nie an Vampire geglaubt. In diesem neuen Fall jedoch scheint es, als müssten die drei berühmten Detektive aus Rocky Beach ihre Meinung ändern ...

Die drei Jungen sind zu einem Ausflug in die Santa Monica Mountains aufgebrochen. Doch gegen Abend werden sie von einem Unwetter überrascht, weshalb sie in dem kleinen Dorf Yonderwood Zuflucht suchen wollen.

Das Dorf scheint jedoch unbewohnt. Alle Häuser stehen leer, sind aber unbeschädigt und wurden sorgfältig verschlossen. Schließlich finden die drei Detektive doch einige Einwohner in dem Gasthaus "The Golden Bear". Die Leute sind allerdings recht unfreundlich, und merkwürdigerweise hängen überall im Gastraum Kreuze und Knoblauchketten herum.

Was geht hier vor? Von Josy, einem hübschen Mädchen, bei dem sie schließlich Unterschlupf finden, erfahren Sie den Grund dafür: die Menschen in dem Ort glauben, dass in Yonderwood ein Vampir umgeht!

Die drei ??? nehmen die Ermittlungen auf und bald überschlagen sich die Ereignisse. Die Tochter des Wirtes wird scheinbar von dem Vampir heimgesucht, eine mannsgroße Fledermaus schwebt nachts durch das Dorf, in einige der leer stehenden Häuser wurde eingebrochen und auf dem Friedhof liegt ein berühmt-berüchtigter Verbrecher begraben ...

Als die drei Jungen weiterforschen, verdichtet sich ein schrecklicher Verdacht: könnte es sein, dass die Bewohner von Yonderwood der Rache eines Mannes zum Opfer fallen sollen, der das Dorf vor über

100 Jahren gegründet hat? Ein Mann, der aus Transsylvanien stammt, der Heimat des Grafen Dracula? Und will er sich an allen rächen oder hat er einen Gehilfen unter den Einwohnern?

Das Geheimnis liegt tief unten in der Gruft der Kirche, doch als die drei Jungen dorthin vordringen, schließt sich der geheime Eingang und sie werden lebendig begraben. Und bald ist Mitternacht ...

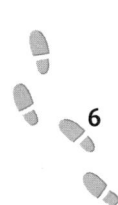

Auftretende Personen

Justus Jonas:
Justus ist der Anführer und der Erste Detektiv der drei ???. Er hat ein phänomenales Gedächtnis, spricht meist in sehr gewählten Worten und trägt ein paar Pfunde zu viel mit sich herum. Justus lebt bei seinem Onkel Titus und seiner Tante Mathilda, die ein Gebrauchtwarencenter in Rocky Beach haben.

Peter Shaw:
Peter ist der zweite Detektiv. Er ist sehr sportlich, hochgewachsen und fast immer gut gelaunt. Im Gegensatz zu Justus ist Peter nicht ganz überzeugt, dass es für alle Phänomene eine logische Erklärung gibt. Daher ist er lieber etwas vorsichtig, wenn es um unheimliche Ereignisse geht. Bei Mädchen ist er äußerst beliebt, aber manchmal etwas abergläubisch und ängstlich.

Bob Andrews:
Bob, der dritte Detektiv, ist für Recherchen und das Archiv zuständig. Das bedeutet, dass er in der Bibliothek und im Internet Informationen sammelt und die Fälle der drei ??? dokumentiert. Bob ist sehr gewissenhaft. Er interessiert sich für Rockmusik und liest gerne. Er ist ein ruhiger Zeitgenosse und sehr vernünftig.

Josy McDonaghough:
In ihrem Auftrag nehmen sich die drei ??? der merkwürdigen Vorgänge in Yonderwood an. Sie ist 16 Jahre, bildhübsch und verdreht den dreien zunächst ganz schön den Kopf.

Elenor McDonaghough:
Josys Oma. Sie ist eine herzensgute, süße alte Frau, die sich jedoch manchmal ein wenig wunderlich verhält.

Jonathan und Miles Black:
Der Bürgermeister von Yonderwood und sein schlaffer Sohn.

Otis und Mary Stamper:
Er ist der bullige Wirt des "Golden Bear" und sie seine zarte Tochter, die dort bedient.

Pfarrer Clark:
Der Geistliche des Ortes, dessen Kirche ein erstaunliches Geheimnis birgt.

Homer Diesel:
Ein verbitterter Mann, der sich selbst als Lebenskünstler ausgibt.

Klara Kowalski:
Eine schwarzhaarige Frau mittleren Alters, die sich abenteuerlich kleidet und in enger Verbindung zu überirdischen Mächten steht.

Sylvester Pound:
Ein ehemaliger Schauspieler mit wehendem weißem Haar, der sehr von sich überzeugt ist.

Alexandru Zelea:
Ein Toter aus Transsylvanien.

1. The Ghost Town

"Here lies Peter Shaw, brilliant investigator[1], king of lock pickers[2] and the heartthrob[3] of many girls. He dedicated his short life to fighting for justice[4]."

"Super, Justus!" laughs Bob. "That's great! We'll write that on his tombstone[5]."

"Ha, ha, ha! You are soooo funny. Can you even imagine how much that hurt?" Peter complains[6].

Bob grins and says, "Or how about: 'in the end, he went to the dogs?'"

He points up at the cliff[7] which Peter has just run into.

"Wow! The top of the cliff really looks like a sheep dog!" Justus says.

Bob shakes his head. "More like a boxer[8]."

Peter sighs[9]. "Great, I almost get a concussion[10] and you talk about different kinds of dogs." he rubs[11] his head.

Justus laughs.

"Oh, come on. By the time you get married, everything will be OK."

"Ha ha, very funny," Peter grumbles[12].

---

1 investigator: Ermittler
2 lock picker: Schlossknacker
3 heartthrob: Schwarm
4 he dedicated his life to fighting for justice: er widmete sein Leben dem Kampf um Gerechtigkeit
5 tombstone: Grabstein
6 to complain: sich beschweren
7 cliff: Klippe
8 boxer: Boxer (Hunderasse)
9 to sigh: seufzen
10 concussion: Gehirnerschütterung
11 to rub: reiben
12 to grumble: murren

The Three Investigators are going on a weekend trip. They want to relax, not think of school and not solve any tricky cases[1], no radio or TV, nothing. To do that, they have gone a few miles inland up into the Santa Monica Mountains.

It happened during a climb. Peter, The Three Investigators' ace sportsman, slipped[2] on some bushes and hit a cliff. A large bump will remain as a souvenir.

They climb[3] for a while longer. The three boys make their way up the hill past dried up trees, bushes, through loose stones and sometimes bare rocks[4]. Sometimes they even have to crawl on all fours[5], but they manage it at last.

"Oh man!" Bob grunts[6] and sits down on the small plateau. "It was pretty steep[7] coming up here."

"But the view is fantastic!"

Peter points to the west, where the Pacific lies in the setting sun[8]. "And over there! A waterfall! Isn't that cute[9]?"

"How romantic!" Justus grins. "But as for cute, Bob, can you please look on the map and check the name of the village down there?" The First Investigator points east towards a small place in a narrow valley[10]. It seems[11] to be about half an hour away and has about forty houses.

"If it's even on the map," answers Bob and looks in his rucksack for the tourist map. When he finds it, he opens it and lays it out on the sandy ground. "That must be it," he says a few minutes later. "That

1 to solve tricky cases: knifflige Fälle lösen
2 to slip: ausrutschen
3 to climb: klettern
4 bare rocks: nackte Felsen
5 to crawl on all fours: auf allen Vieren krabbeln
6 to groan: ächzen
7 pretty steep: ziemlich steil
8 setting sun: untergehende Sonne
9 cute: süß
10 narrow valley: enges Tal
11 to seem: scheinen

here is the brook[1], which plunges over the cliffs[2] over there," Bob points over to the waterfall. "And if I am not wrong, then this small spot here is the place." The Third Investigator points at a dark red rectangle[3] and looks at the map more closely[4]. "It's called ... one moment ... Yonderwood."

"Yonderwood?" Justus looks at his friend in surprise.

"Funny name," Peter says, "Yonderwood, hmmmmm."

"Oh well," Justus shrugs[5], "Whatever it is, let's go down there. We'll buy a few things for supper or perhaps there's even an inn[6] or some such place. Then we don't even have to warm up our food ourselves. Somehow I don't feel like eating soup from a gas stove[7]. What do you think?"

"Good idea," Bob agrees[8].

"If you like," Peter says, "Even if it's not very authentic[9] wandering through the mountains with a rucksack and then ending up in some restaurant eating steak and fries."

"Maybe not authentic," answers Justus, and grins at Peter, "but more tasty!"

However, when the three boys stand at the village entrance[10] an hour later, it doesn't seem as if they can get even a piece of bread, let alone[11] steak and fries. The deserted[12] place lies before them in the evening light and there isn't any sign that anyone lives there. Even

1 brook: Bach
2 which plunges over the cliffs: der sich über die Klippen stürzt
3 rectangle: Rechteck
4 to look at the map more closely: sich die Karte genauer anschauen
5 to shrug: mit den Schultern zucken
6 inn: Gaststätte
7 gas stove: Gaskocher, Gasherd
8 to agree: zustimmen
9 authentic: authentisch
10 entrance: Eingang
11 let alone: geschweige denn
12 deserted: verlassen

worse, a thunderstorm is rolling in with sinister rumbling[1]. Somewhere, a door slams[2] in the wind, which howls[3] through the main street.

"Well guys, I don't like saying this," whispers[4] Peter, "You know what they call places like this."

"A ... dump[5]?" Bob asks.

"No," Peter shakes his head. "They call this a ghost town[6]!"

Detective Question

Why does Peter call Yonderwood a Ghost Town?

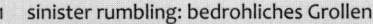

1 sinister rumbling: bedrohliches Grollen
2 to slam: knallen
3 to howl: heulen
4 to whisper: flüstern
5 dump: Dreckloch
6 ghost town: Geisterstadt

2. Dark Memory

The first bolt of lightning[1] flashes[2] across the sky which is slowly getting darker and darker in the east. Shortly after that, there is a bang, followed by a deep rumble[3]. It almost sounds as if a gigantic cannon ball is rolling down the mountain.
"The thunderstorm is getting close!" Justus says matter-of-factly[4]. "And fast! We should find shelter[5] somewhere. It could get very uncomfortable. Let's wait inside one of those houses until the worst is over."
"You want to go inside one of the ghost houses?" Peter asks, horrified[6].
"You are welcome to[7] stay here," Justus answers. "Then we'll get you later and wring you out[8]."
"You'd better[9] put on a hat!" Bob says to Peter with a grin.
Peter rolls his eyes. "One day," he says, "you'll see that there are powers in heaven and earth that can't be logically explained. And then you will be lying in the dust[10] in front of me and begging for forgiveness[11] because you didn't take me seriously[12]."
Justus and Bob laugh and then the three boys run towards the first house on the street.

---

1 bolt of lightning: Blitz
2 to flash: blitzen
3 rumble: Grollen
4 matter-of-factly: sachlich
5 shelter: Unterschlupf
6 horrified: entsetzt
7 you are welcome to stay here: du kannst gern hierbleiben
8 to wring out: auswringen
9 you had better: du solltest besser/lieber
10 dust: Staub
11 to beg for forgiveness: um Vergebung betteln, um Verzeihung bitten
12 to take someone seriously: jemanden ernst nehmen

The windows look black and paint is peeling¹ from the doors.
Justus knocks at the door three times. "Hello? Anyone there?"
The boys wait for a few seconds, but no movement.
"I can't see anyone," says Peter, who is trying to look inside the house.
"Heigh ho?" Justus tries again. But everything is silent. Finally, he shrugs and pushes down the door handle² carefully.
"Locked³!" he says in surprise and rattles⁴ the door a little. "They've locked it!"
"Peter, do you have your lockpicks⁵ with you?" Bob asks.
The Second Investigator is responsible⁶ for locks of all kinds. "Dammit," he swears⁷. "I think I left them in my other trousers. Sorry!"
"Don't worry. There are enough other empty houses," Justus says and runs towards a house on the other side of the street.
Meanwhile, fat raindrops fall, hitting the ground hard. The gaps⁸ between the flashes of lightning which light up the ghost village grow shorter and shorter.
Even if the houses are deserted, they haven't been abandoned hastily.⁹ Every one in which the boys try their luck has been carefully locked up when its occupants¹⁰ moved out.
"Such bad luck!" Peter looks out at the rain. "Should we break a window and climb in?"
"Perhaps it would be best." Bob agrees.

---

1 to peel: *hier* – abblättern
2 door handle: Türgriff
3 locked: abgeschlossen
4 to rattle: *hier* – rütteln
5 lockpick: Dietrich
6 responsible: verantwortlich
7 to swear: fluchen
8 gap: Lücke
9 abandoned hastily: schnell verlassen/zurückgelassen
10 occupant: Bewohner

"That won't be necessary[1]." Justus points across the street. "Take a look there."
Peter and Bob turn around and stare through the rain at the other side of the street.
"I'll be damned![2]"
"Who would have thought it[3]! There seems to be life here!"
On the other side of the street there is a house which on first sight seems no different to the others. It has two floors[4] and seems just as deserted as all the other houses in the street. However, when the First Investigator looks closely, he discovers[5] an important difference: light is coming through the closed shutters[6]!
"And it's even a restaurant, if I am reading the sign correctly." Justus points to a golden sign above the door of the house. On the sign, there is a bear that's lifting a tankard to its snout[7].
"Let's go," Peter says. "Perhaps we can still get our steak and fries."
The three boys run across the street through the rain. Once they get there, they look up at the sign.
"'The Golden Bear,'" Bob reads. He raises[8] his finger to his lips. "There are a few people inside. I hear voices."
"Let's go in," Justus says, and rubs his hands. "Otherwise we'll drown[9] out here."
The First Investigator pushes the door handle down and opens the door. Peter goes past him into a hallway[10] which is separated[11] from

---

1 that won't be necessary: nicht nötig, das wird nicht nötig sein
2 I'll be damned – Ausruf des Erstaunens (umgangssprachlich)
3 who would have thought it: wer hätte das gedacht
4 floor: *hier* – Stockwerk
5 to discover: entdecken
6 shutters: Fensterläden
7 that's lifting a tankard to his snout: der einen Krug zu seiner Schnauze hebt
8 to raise: heben
9 to drown: ertrinken
10 hallway: Flur, Diele
11 separated: getrennt

the rest of the restaurant by a heavy black curtain[1]. Bob follows him, and as Justus closes the door behind him, the noise of the rain dies down[2]. But the sounds from the restaurant suddenly stop, too. Only a clock is ticking.

"What's happening now?" Bob looks at his friends in surprise.

Justus shakes his head, confused[3]. Peter opens the curtain and lets Bob and Justus go through. Then he goes inside.

"Good evening everyone!" he calls cheerfully. "What horrible weather outside. You wouldn't even send a dog out …"

Peter stops suddenly and stares into the room with his mouth open.

Justus and Bob do the same. They are speechless[4] and just look at each other in confusion.

However, it isn't the six or seven guests who surprise them. None of them answer Peter's greeting. But it isn't that which troubles[5] The Three Investigators.

It is the restaurant's unusual décor[6]. A décor which is simply … strange. On every wall there hangs at least[7] one big cross and everywhere in the room, really everywhere, there are never ending chains[8] of … garlic[9]! Chains of garlic hang from every lamp, there is garlic on the tables and chains of garlic even decorate the crosses on the walls. It looks silly but at the same time very strange and somehow alarming[10]. It reminds the boys of something spooky[11], something that they

---

1 curtain: Vorhang
2 to die down: *hier* – verstummen
3 confused: verwirrt
4 speechless: sprachlos
5 to trouble: bekümmern, irritieren
6 décor: Dekor, Einrichtung
7 at least: mindestens
8 chain: Kette
9 garlic: Knoblauch
10 alarming: beunruhigend
11 spooky: gruselig

have seen before. They just don't remember at once where and when.
But then Peter remembers. Suddenly he knows where he has seen all that before, and he bursts out: "But this looks like a bad vampire film! Crosses and garlic everywhere! The only thing missing is a man with a black cape and long, bloody teeth!"
Suddenly the waitress[1] lets out a scream and drops her tray[2].

Detective Question

Why do you think the shutters of the inn are closed, even though there are people there?

---

1 waitress: Kellnerin
2 tray: Tablett

3. The Secret of Yonderwood

"What do you want?" an unfriendly voice asks at that moment. It belongs to the innkeeper[1] behind the bar. The man glares[2] at The Three Investigators.

"Oh, we wanted to ask … if we can buy a few small things here." Justus has quickly changed his mind[3]. Even if they sell the best steak in the whole of California here, he doesn't want it. He doesn't want to stay in this strange restaurant with these hostile[4] people any longer than necessary.

"In the drugstore[5]," the landlord grunts. "Over there on the other side of the street, a few houses further on." Then he turns away quickly, and starts to clean his glasses.

"Thank you," Justus answers shortly. He grabs[6] Peter and Bob and they leave the bar together.

"Oh boy! What nice people in there!" Bob complains when they are outside. "And the atmosphere! Simply wonderful! We definitely have to invite them all to our next party!"

Justus nods, but seems more serious[7] than angry.

"These people really behaved very strangely. And also I thought the décor was strange[8]. Why do they decorate their restaurant with garlic and crosses?" The First Investigator stops, shakes his head and says, "I have the feeling that something's wrong here. Apart from that,[9]

---

1 innkeeper: Wirt
2 to glare: wütend anstarren
3 to change one's mind: die Meinung ändern
4 hostile: feindselig
5 drugstore: Drogerie
6 to grab: packen
7 serious: ernst
8 weird: merkwürdig, seltsam
9 apart from that: außerdem

I also had the feeling that they were under some great … strain[1], as if something troubles them a lot."

"I agree," Peter says. "Guys, I have the feeling that they're afraid of something! Horribly afraid!"

None of the boys speaks for a few seconds. All three of them just stare out at the rain.

"Let's look for the drugstore," Justus says quietly and pulls up the collar[2] of his jacket. "Hopefully it's open."

One after the other, the three boys run out into the pouring[3] rain. Soon their clothes are completely wet.

"Where's this damned[4] shop?" Peter growls. But his voice is drowned out[5] by a big clap of thunder[6].

"There!" Justus says, running ahead of Peter and Bob. "That looks like a drugstore to me. A big shop window and a glass door. But the blinds[7] are pulled down."

"Ring the bell then!" Bob says. "Or knock! I want to get in. I'm already completely wet!"

Justus finds a bell next to the door and rings it.

Soon after that, light shines through the blinds. "Yes, yes, I'm coming!" The Three Investigators hear a youthful[8] voice inside the shop. Then the door opens and light pours[9] out into the wet darkness.

"Well! Who are you?" A girl of about sixteen with big brown eyes and thick black hair that curls round her exceptionally[10] pretty face looks at The Three Investigators in surprise.

---

1 strain: Anspannung
2 collar: Kragen
3 pouring: strömend
4 damned: verdammt
5 to be drowned out: übertönt werden
6 clap of thunder: Donnerschlag
7 blinds: Rolladen, Jalousien
8 youthful: jugendlich, jung
9 to pour: *hier* – sich ergießen
10 exceptionally: außerordentlich

Justus pushes his wet hair away from his face. "Hello, I'm Justus, – Justus Jonas, and these are my friends Bob Andrews and Peter Shaw."

"The people in The Golden Bear sent us over," Peter explains. "They thought we could maybe buy a few things here. At the moment we could really use a few towels[1]."

The girl laughs. "Come in!" she says and steps aside. "We are actually not open but I can't really send you away again looking so pitiful[2]. By the way, I'm Josy McDonaghough."

"Thanks, that's really very nice, thanks," says Justus.

"Great!" Peter adds.

Bob shakes himself like a wet dog. "Saved[3]!"

Josy shuts the shop door and goes behind the sales counter[4]. "So what can I do for you now? What are you doing here in this lonely[5] part of the world? Tourists hardly ever[6] come here and especially not in such bad weather."

"We're not really tourists," Justus answers. "We're from Rocky Beach and wanted to spend the weekend here in the mountains."

"From Rocky Beach? I think I've heard of that before," Josy says thoughtfully[7].

Over the next few minutes, the three boys tell Josy about their planned mountain tour, about Rocky Beach and of course about their detective office[8] . In turn, they find out that Josy lives here with her grandmother Eleanora, who owns[9] the drugstore and that her parents, just like Justus' parents, died in an accident. Josy also tells them

---

1 towel: Handtuch
2 pitiful: erbärmlich, bemitleidenswert
3 saved: gerettet
4 sales counter: Verkaufstresen
5 lonely: einsam
6 hardly ever: fast nie
7 thoughtfully: nachdenklich
8 detective office: Detektivbüro
9 to own: besitzen

that Yonderwood is really as much of a dump as it seems. But there is something that Justus really wants to talk about.

"Tell me," he begins, "the restaurant over there, The Golden Bear. Is there some unusual custom[1] which we don't know about? Why is the décor there so strange?"

Suddenly Josy seems to grow reserved[2] and unfriendly.

"I ... I don't want to talk about it," she answers quietly.

The Three Investigators look at one another. "Josy," Bob begins and gives her an understanding[3] smile, "we really don't want to intrude[4]. But we've noticed[5] some strange things. There's something fishy[6] going on."

"Something fishy?" Josy snorts[7]. "Maybe you see it like that! But it's really too silly."

Justus looks at Josy. "You say that the situation is silly, but all the people here in Yonderwood seem to be very afraid of it. And even you don't really seem to think it's funny."

Josy covers[8] her face with her hands.

"It's absurd," she says, "and also embarrassing[9]. But also somehow spooky and frightening, although I don't believe all the nonsense[10] those people over there want us to believe."

She nods in the direction of The Golden Bear and adds: "I just *don't* want to believe this nonsense!"

"What nonsense?" Bob wants to know.

"What do they want you to believe, Josy?" Peter asks.

---

1 unusual custom: ungewöhnlicher Brauch
2 reserved: reserviert
3 understanding: *hier* – verständnisvoll
4 to intrude: sich aufdrängen
5 to notice: bemerken
6 there's something fishy going on: hier ist etwas faul
7 to snort: schnauben
8 to cover: bedecken
9 embarrassing: peinlich
10 nonsense: Unsinn

Josy is silent for a moment. Then she slowly shakes her curly head, laughs in a forced way¹ and begins: "Since about eight weeks ago, one resident² after another has left Yonderwood. Until a short time ago, a hundred people lived here. Now there are exactly ten. They, too, won't stay here much longer if everything continues³ like this. And everyone who left did so for a reason which I will never, never, never believe, because it's too silly and embarrassing and …," Josy pauses, "creepy⁴." Almost in a whisper, she says, "They say that there is … a vampire in Yonderwood!"

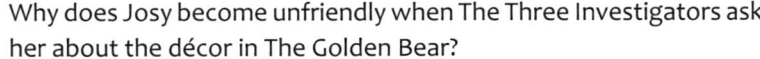

Detective Question

Why does Josy become unfriendly when The Three Investigators ask her about the décor in The Golden Bear?

---

1 in a forced way: gezwungen
2 resident: Einwohner
3 to continue like this: so weitergehen
4 creepy: unheimlich

4. Seas of Blood

"Oh God," Peter says, "I was right!"

"Slowly please!" Justus raises his hands. "Don't talk too soon, guys[1]. Stay calm!" He turns to Josy and asks, "Did you say a vampire? There's supposed to be[2] a vampire in your village?"

Josy looks unhappy. "That's what they say, yes."

"But how did you get this silly idea? A vampire is an imaginary figure, a myth[3], a mere fantasy[4]! There aren't any vampires!"

"You don't have to tell me that!" answers Josy. "But it seems like there is one here. And I'm frightened because of that!"

The Three Investigators are disturbed[5]. Something very strange is happening in Yonderwood.

"And … and what are these signs?" Bob asks carefully after a while.

"As I said, it began about eight weeks ago." Josy looks past The Three Investigators. "At first it happened to old Black, our mayor[6]. He woke up one morning and found that his whole pillow[7] was full of blood. At first he thought he'd hurt himself in his sleep. But when Dr. Pleasance examined[8] him, at first he couldn't find a wound[9] which could have caused[10] so much blood. Then he found two puncture wounds[11] next to each other." Josy pauses for a moment, "On his neck."

"The bite wounds!" Peter looks at Josy with horror. "Typical wounds from a vampire's bite! They always bite the neck!"

---

1 guys: Jungs, Leute
2 supposed to be: angeblich
3 a myth: ein Mythos
4 a mere fantasy: bloβe Einbildung
5 disturbed: beunruhigt
6 mayor: Bürgermeister
7 pillow: Kissen
8 to examine: untersuchen
9 wound: Wunde
10 which could have caused: die hätte verursachen können
11 puncture: Einstich

"Peter!" Justus shakes his head. "There's no such thing as a vampire! Do you hear? Is that clear?"

"That's what you say!" Peter answers.

Josy continues: "Everyone in the village wondered what could have caused Jonathan Black's unusual wounds. Some people thought that he'd been bitten by giant mosquitoes, others thought that the old man was wearing a hairnet[1] at night and some hair pins[2] had hurt his neck. But a few days later something happened which stopped the stupid jokes." Josy stops for a minute. She shivers[3]. "First two more people woke up in seas of blood and then ... several[4] people saw an enormous bat[5] over the roofs of Yonderwood! It only appears after midnight and is supposed to be as big as a man!"

The Three Investigators are silent. Justus seems skeptical[6]. Bob looks uneasy, and Peter is nervous.

"Vampires ... can turn[7] themselves into bats," says the Second Investigator in a trembling voice[8].

"Hm," Justus says thoughtfully. "Let's not worry about the batman for a minute. Who was bitten next, Josy? Although I really can't believe that a vampire's bite was the cause of the wounds."

"Mrs. Davenport was the next one. The poor thing! After she was honoured for her special services[9] to Yonderwood, she woke up the next morning in her own blood and had these horrible marks[10] on her neck." Josy shakes her head. "She left Yonderwood on the same day and now lives with her daughter near Santa Monica."

---

1 hair net: Haarnetz
2 hair pins: Haarnadeln
3 to shiver: zittern, schaudern
4 several: einige
5 an enormous bat: eine riesige Fledermaus
6 skeptical: skeptisch
7 turn themselves into: sich verwandeln in
8 in a trembling voice: mit zitternder Stimme
9 honoured for special services: für besondere Dienste geehrt
10 mark: Mal, Spur

"And the next one?" Justus looks at Josy intently[1].

"Patricia Hamilton. The morning after her birthday, she came out of the house screaming, covered[2] in her own blood. She's in Malibu now."

"That is simply horrible!" Peter comments[3].

"And the rest of the residents moved away one after the other?"

"Yes, one after the other," says Josy sadly.

"First it was only a few who left, but the more people left, the more frightened those who stayed became. Now there are only ten residents left, plus grandma and me."

"And why are just these ten here?" asks Bob.

"Everyone had some different important reason," Josy says. "But they are all frightened of the vampire."

"Everyone believes in the vampire except you," Peter interrupts[4].

Josy smiles weakly. "It makes no difference whether I believe in it or not. I have to stay here until I can convince[5] grandmother to move away with me. At her age, I can't leave her alone here. And she will not leave here."

She turns away and closes her eyes. But The Three Investigators notice the tears rolling down her cheeks. It is clear that the situation is very difficult for her.

"If only it would stop!" Josy suddenly shouts." I can't take it anymore[6]! I would do anything if this madness could be stopped at last! Anything!" Then she starts sobbing uncontrollably[7].

---

1 intently: aufmerksam, gespannt
2 covered in blood: blutüberströmt
3 to comment: bemerken, kommentieren
4 to interrupt: unterbrechen
5 to convince: überzeugen
6 I can't take it anymore: ich kann es nicht mehr ertragen
7 to sob uncontrollably: untröstlich schluchzen

Detective Question

If there really is a vampire, it is strange that there is blood everywhere. Why?

5. The Vampire Hunters[1]

Justus gives Josy a tissue[2]. "First of all, the only thing you have to do is get us a room here in Yonderwood."
Josy blows her nose and looks confused. "You want me to get you a room?" she asks in surprise. "I – I ... don't understand. Why?"
The First Investigator puts his hand into the pocket of his jacket and gives Josy one of their business cards[3]. "That's why!"

> The Three Investigators
> We take on any case
> First Investigator Justus Jonas
> Second Investigator Peter Shaw
> Research and Archives Bob Andrews

Josy looks at the card while Justus continues[4], "If you like, we can examine what is going on in this village a bit more closely. This looks like a new case for The Three Investigators."
"That's right," Peter agrees, although he feels a bit worried.
"I think that would be really great," Josy bursts out[5]. "I really think that's cool. Then I wouldn't feel so ... helpless[6] and alone anymore." She looks at the three boys gratefully[7].
"Well, then we can start. Let's pull the batman's teeth," Bob says.
Josy smiles. "And I also have a room for you. Upstairs under the roof. It's not a Hilton suite but it's clean and dry. But there aren't any beds."

---
1 hunter: Jäger
2 tissue: (Papier)Taschentuch
3 business card: Visitenkarte
4 to continue: fortfahren
5 to burst out: herausplatzen
6 helpless: hilflos
7 gratefully: dankbar

"No problem," Bob answers. "We have our sleeping bags and insulated mats[1] with us."

"Well … come along!"

Josy takes The Three Investigators to their room, which is two floors higher up under the roof.

"I will call you for breakfast," she tells them. Then she says, "Goodnight, and thank you once again."

She closes the door behind her gently[2]. Peter waits until the sounds of her steps on the stairs have died down. Then he puts his sleeping bag on the floor.

"Well, fantastic! Instead of sitting somewhere under the open sky by a campfire, grilling potatoes and howling at the moon[3], we are locking ourselves in a small room in case[4] a vampire tries to suck[5] our blood tonight. And tomorrow we might even be chasing this guy[6]." Peter looks around the room. "Perhaps we should borrow[7] a little of that stuff from the restaurant and hang it up in here."

Justus says, "It was the right thing to help Josy, and besides, may I remind you[8] that it's raining outside … "

He points to the window against which the rain is beating[9]. "So in any case we couldn't have howled at the moon."

"Hm," Peter grunts, while Bob makes himself comfortable on the floor. "But how are we going to chase a vampire? Tomorrow, should we take some hammers and nails and break open[10] every coffin[11] in the village to check if a man with sharp teeth is lying inside?"

---

1 insulated mat: Isomatte
2 gently: sanft, leise
3 to howl at the moon: den Mond anheulen
4 in case: falls/für den Fall, dass
5 to suck: saugen
6 we might be chasing this guy: wir jagen diesem Typen vielleicht hinterher
7 to borrow: sich ausleihen
8 may I remind you: darf ich dich daran erinnern
9 against which the rain is beating: gegen das der Regen trommelt
10 to break open: aufbrechen
11 coffin: Sarg

"No," says the First Investigator. "Next, we have to find out what exactly happened. And we should get to know every single resident who is still here. Who knows? Perhaps this could lead to the first clue[1]."

"Do you think one of them is behind all this?" Bob asks.

"That is possible," answers Justus. "On the other hand, it's also possible that someone who is no longer living here is responsible for the events[2]."

"Wait a minute!" protests Peter. "Events! Happenings! Has it occurred to you[3] that there could be dangerous powers at work[4] here?"

"Oh, Peter!" Justus sighs. "Normally you're such a clever guy. Why don't you trust[5] your common sense[6] instead of always embracing the next superstition[7]?"

Peter doesn't answer and only grins at Justus. He often has discussions like this with him and he knows that he won't be able to convince[8] the First Investigator . Justus will never doubt the laws of reason[9] and common sense. Peter knows Justus feels that way. But he is sure that one day Justus' eyes will be opened, and maybe that day isn't too far off!

Detective Question

Why is it smart for Justus to try to find out more about the village and its residents?

1 clue: Anhaltspunkt, Hinweis
2 event: Ereignis
3 to occur to someone: jemandem einfallen
4 there could be dangerous powers at work: es könnten gefährliche Mächte am Werk sein
5 to trust: vertrauen (auf)
6 common sense: gesunder Menschenverstand
7 embracing the next superstition: sich dem nächstbesten Aberglauben hingeben
8 won't be able to convince: wird nicht überzeugen können
9 the laws of reason: die Gesetze der Vernunft

6. The Ten Little Indians

Josy wakes The Three Investigators soon after sunrise. The Second Investigator feels very tired. The whole night he dreamt of enormous bats and bloody teeth.

The tired boys go downstairs and help Josy make breakfast. They are relieved[1] that there isn't any garlic in the kitchen. However, a cross hangs on the wall and a framed Bible verse[2] hangs over the mantelpiece[3]. But the McDonaghoughs don't seem to be superstitious[4].

"First Maccabees[5] 2, 60," Justus reads the Bible verse. "Because Daniel was innocent, he was snatched out of the lion's jaw[6]." He turns to Josy, surprised.

Josy shrugs, "That's been hanging there for ages[7]. Nobody knows why. I believe it comes from grandmother's great-grandfather."

"Your family has been in Yonderwood that long?" asks Peter.

"Yes, *too* long," answers Josy.

At breakfast, the three boys meet Josy's grandmother. Mrs. Eleanora McDonaghough is a very nice and kind[8] old lady. She chats away cheerfully[9] and tells the boys about her past.

But sometimes she seems a little confused. She mixes up[10] The Three Investigators, puts the teapot[11] into the refrigerator and says she is looking forward to Christmas. In August …

---

1 relieved: erleichtert
2 a framed Bible verse: ein gerahmter Bibelvers
3 mantelpiece: Kaminsims
4 superstitious: abergläubisch
5 Maccabees: Makkabäer
6 snatched out of the lion's jaw: dem Maul des Löwen entrissen
7 for ages: seit Ewigkeiten
8 kind: freundlich, liebenswürdig
9 to chat away cheerfully: munter plaudern
10 to mix up: durcheinanderbringen
11 teapot: Teekanne

"My grandmother is sometimes a bit confused," says Josy after breakfast. "I should have[1] warned you. But she's an absolute treasure[2] and I love her a lot."
Justus empties his cup. "She's really very nice." Then he asks Josy, "Would it be possible to get to know the other residents of Yonderwood? It would be really important for our investigation, and we need their help."
Josy begins to clear the table[3]. "And how would you like to go about it[4]?" she asks. "I mean, do you want me to introduce you to every one of the residents who is still here?"
Peter grins. "We could visit everyone and say: 'Hello, how are you? By the way, we are the new vampire hunters. Could we perhaps look at your teeth?'"
Justus forces a smile[5] before he turns to Josy again. "Do you think you could get all the villagers together tonight in The Golden Bear? Tell them you have something important to say to them!"
Josy raises her eyebrows[6]. "And what shall I say?"
"Tell them that you've found someone to solve the village's problems. Tell them we heard about what has been happening in Yonderwood and that we have a lot of experience[7] with these kinds of things. And then you can introduce us."
"Hm," murmurs[8] Peter. "And what would that be good for?"
"Two things," answers Justus. "For one thing, we get to know all the residents. And perhaps we can make the vampire a bit nervous."
"You mean we rattle[9] whoever is behind it?" Bob guesses.

---

1 I should have: ich hätte ... sollen
2 treasure: Schatz
3 to clear the table: den Tisch abräumen
4 to go about it: *hier* – vorgehen
5 to force a smile: sich ein Lächeln abringen
6 she raises her eyebrows: sie zieht die Augenbrauen hoch
7 a lot of experience: viel Erfahrung
8 to murmur: murmeln
9 to rattle: *hier* – verunsichern

"Absolutely right," Justus says. "And perhaps he will make a mistake that leads us to him."
"That only works if the vampire is one of the residents," Peter comments. "And even if that's the case, it can backfire[1]."
"What do you mean?" Josy wants to know.
"Perhaps if we open our mouths too far, we'll be the vampire's next victims[2]."

Just before seven, all the residents are gathered[3] in The Golden Bear. However, the three detectives quickly realize[4] that they aren't going to have an easy time. Josy introduces them one by one, and then it is the three boys' turn. They can feel the villagers' suspicion[5], which is like the fear which they already noticed the evening before.
"We'll only make the vampire more angry!" Otis Stamper, the landlord, says. "Let's leave him alone! Maybe he'll forget about us and then go away."
"You're right, Otis, absolutely right!" Sylvester Pound, a has-been actor[6] with snow-white hair shouts.
"Let's not make him angry!" Miles Black, the mayor's son, agrees. He is a pale[7], unassuming[8] young man in his mid-twenties, who still lives in his father's house.
Pastor Clark, on the other hand, does not say much. And a man called Homer Diesel, who introduces himself as a *bon viveur*[9], also remains quiet. Klara Kowalski, a black-haired, middle-aged[10] lady who is dressed

---

1 to backfire: nach hinten losgehen
2 victim: Opfer
3 to be gathered: versammelt sein
4 to realize: erkennen, einsehen
5 suspicion: Misstrauen, Argwohn
6 a has-been actor: ein Schauspieler, der die beste Zeit hinter sich hat
7 pale: blass
8 unassuming: unscheinbar, unauffällig
9 bon viveur: französisch für Lebenskünstler
10 middle-aged: mittleren Alters

in unusual coloured rags[1] can't say anything. She just stares at the three boys the whole time.

"Now, my dear people," Jonathan Black, the mayor, says, "I am of quite a different opinion. I think we should take every bit of help we can get. Should we really wait until the vampire visits every one of us, one after the other?"

The other residents listen to him. "This all somehow reminds me of the mystery[2] 'Ten Little Indians' by Agatha Christie," whispers Peter. "There were also ten people at first and one by one[3] they are killed!"

"What nonsense!" Justus answers.

Black clears his throat[4] and continues. "But let's suppose[5] these Three Investigators are right and there is something quite different behind all this – isn't it then in our interest to clear up the matter[6] as soon as possible? Have a look around! Nearly all our friends and fellow residents[7] have moved away. Our village is dying! We have to do something!"

Miles Black lifts his glass. "Father is right. Let's drink to the three boys. It can't get worse than it is at the moment. And perhaps they really can help us."

Everyone raises their glass and Miles smiles at the waitress Mary – who is Stamper's daughter – encouragingly[8]. The Three Investigators recognize[9] her at once – she was so terribly frightened the evening before. Mary smiles back shyly and sips[10] her lemonade.

---

1 coloured rags: bunte Fetzen
2 (murder) mystery: Krimi, Kriminalroman
3 one by one: einer nach dem anderen
4 clears his throat: räuspert sich
5 let's suppose: lasst uns mal annehmen
6 to clear up the matter: die Sache klären
7 fellow residents: Mitbewohner
8 encouragingly: aufmunternd, ermutigend
9 recognize: wiedererkennen
10 to sip something: an etwas nippen

Only Diesel doesn't lift his glass. He looks for some money in his wallet, throws it on the table and gets up.

"You are going to get *all* of us killed!" he angrily hisses[1] at Jonathan Black, stressing[2] the word 'all'.

Then he pushes his chair to the side noisily and walks to the door.

Detective Question

Why does Justus want to tell the whole village that they are there to catch the vampire?

---

[1] to hiss: zischen
[2] to stress: betonen

7. And Then There Were Nine

"Are you starting that again? Can't you ever stop?" Black hisses at Diesel.

"I know what I know!" Diesel looks at him coldly.

Josy bends closer to The Three Investigators. "Diesel believes that Black is responsible for his wife's death[1]," she whispers.

Jonathan Black shouts, "You are absolutely crazy!"

Mary starts to cry. The two men's fight[2] obviously[3] upsets[4] her.

"Poor little thing," says Sylvester Pound and sighs. "She's just too delicate[5] for this hard world. She always reminds me a little of the great Elvira Lockhead. She was also such a good soul."

"Oh, Sylvester! Spare us[6] your idiotic sayings!" Diesel growls. "Delicate? Don't make me laugh. The girl should find a husband, that's all."

Stamper spins[7] around. "And what's that supposed to mean[8]?" he shouts at Diesel.

Before Homer can answer, Pastor Clark quickly gets up from his chair. "Now my dear brothers and sisters," he says, "it's been a long evening, and we are all a bit irritable[9]. I think we should all go home now."

---

1. to be responsible for something: für etwas verantwortlich sein
2. fight: Streit
3. obviously: offensichtlich
4. to upset someone: jemanden unglücklich machen, jemanden verärgern
5. delicate: zart, empfindlich
6. spare us: verschon uns mit, erspar uns
7. to spin around: herumwirbeln
8. what's that supposed to mean: was soll das heißen
9. irritable: gereizt

Obviously the Pastor's word still carries weight[1] in Yonderwood. One by one, everybody leaves the restaurant. Finally, only Stamper, Josy and the three boys are left in the room.

"My goodness[2]!" Peter says in surprise. "What was that?"

"Homer's wife died in a car accident ages ago when she went into town with Jonathan Black," Josy explains. "Black was hardly hurt but Mrs. Diesel was fatally injured[3]. Even now, Homer hasn't forgiven[4] Black. Even though it was clear that it wasn't his fault[5]. There was a problem with the car."

"And why didn't Homer leave Yonderwood?" asks Bob.

"He loved his wife above everything and didn't want to leave the place where she had lived," answers Josy.

"It's time," Justus looks at the clock and gets up. "We should get ready for the coming night."

"What are you planning to do?" asks Josy in surprise.

"As your visitor only comes out at night and we want to meet him, whether we like it or not, we will have to stay up the next few nights."

The Three Investigators plan to take turns[6] to lie in wait[7] after dark. Perhaps something strange will happen. The three boys get their things from Bob's VW-beetle and are ready to begin.

"And don't forget to put the walkie-talkies on receiving mode[8], OK?" Bob reminds both his friends. "I'll be with you at midnight and wake you, Justus."

"No problem."

---

1 to carry weight: Gewicht haben
2 my goodness: meine Güte
3 fatally injured: tödlich verletzt
4 to forgive: verzeihen
5 it wasn't his fault: es war nicht seine Schuld
6 to take turns: sich abwechseln
7 to lie in wait: auf der Lauer liegen
8 on receiving mode: *hier* – auf Empfang

"See you later!" Bob says and walks in the direction of the village entrance. Justus and Peter go into the house with Josy. They want to sleep as much as possible[1] before they get woken up.

However, on the first night watch[2] nothing interesting happens.

Not even a vampire's shadow is to be seen and no giant bat either. But the next morning, the village and its residents experience fear and horror once again.

Peter is just on his way to the McDonaghough's house to have breakfast when a blood-curdling[3] scream tears through the air[4]!

The Second Investigator spins around and stares at The Golden Bear. At that moment, Mary Stamper runs out of the door! With her hair flying and her white nightgown[5] she looks like a ghost. And the nightgown is completely covered in blood!

"Help!" Peter shouts, as Mary stumbles[6] down the street. Then she collapses[7] in the middle of the street. "HELP! Come here quickly!"

Within a few minutes, the whole village is up and about. They all start talking at once, everybody is shocked and confused. The Three Investigators carry the unconscious[8] girl back into her house and lay her on a sofa.

But as soon as Stamper pushes open the door, he lets out a curse[9]: "Damn! Where are the garlic and the crosses?"

Everyone runs into the room and looks around fearfully. Only The Three Investigators keep a clear head. They call the doctor. Justus

---

1 as much as possible: soviel wie möglich
2 watch: *hier* – Wache
3 blood-curdling: markerschütternd
4 tears through the air: zerreißt die Luft
5 nightgown: Nachthemd
6 to stumble: stolpern
7 to collapse: zusammenbrechen
8 unconscious: bewusstlos
9 to let out a curse: einen Fluch ausstoßen

feels Mary's wrist. "Her pulse is weak but regular[1]." He examines both the wounds on her neck. "She's only unconscious."
"Thank God!" whispers Stamper and wipes the sweat from his forehead[2]. "But I don't understand what happened with the garlic and the crosses. Who put them away?"
"She could only have done that herself," Pound comments. "The vampire can't touch them."
"But why should she?" asks Miles.
"Perhaps he ordered[3] it!" his father says. "We know that Mary is easily influenced[4]."
"Everything is in the kitchen!" Pastor Clark suddenly calls from one of the other rooms. After a quick look into the kitchen, Justus taps Peter and Bob on their shoulders and waves them away from the others.
"What is it?" asks Peter quietly.
Justus looks indecisive[5]. "I just don't really know," he says. "It's all very strange."
"Really?" Peter pretends[6] to be surprised. "You find it strange here? I really didn't expect you to say that."
"It really is exactly as they told us," Justus goes on, thoughtfully. "There are two puncture wounds in the neck. But I can't explain any of this to myself."
"What exactly do you mean?" Bob wants to know.
Justus looks at his friend with surprise. "Have a look around! It looks like the butcher[7] was here. Just look at the bed!"
Peter and Bob look at Mary's bed. The pillow is soaked[8] in blood.

---

1 regular: regelmäßig
2 wipes the sweat from his forehead: wischt sich den Schweiß von seiner Stirn
3 to order: *hier* – befehlen
4 easily influenced: leicht zu beeinflussen
5 indecisive: unentschlossen
6 to pretend: so tun als ob
7 butcher: Metzger
8 soaked in blood: in Blut getränkt

"There's far too much blood here!" Justus says, confused. "The wound is too small for Mary to have lost so much blood from it! But it's there. Where does all this blood come from?" The First Investigator pauses. "And then the whole thing with the garlic and the crosses: that doesn't make sense[1]. It doesn't make any sense at all."

Detective Question

What different explanation can you think of for why the garlic and the crosses aren't in the room anymore?

---

1 it doesn't make sense: es ergibt keinen Sinn

8. Once Bitten, Twice Shy[1]!

Even before the doctor arrives, Mary recovers[2] a little. However, she can't remember anything. Stamper packs a few things together and when the doctor arrives, he and the paramedic[3] help Mary on the way to the ambulance[4].
Homer Diesel takes her hand and says shyly, "Sorry about last night," before the ambulance drives her and her father west, away from Yonderwood.
The other villagers stay in front of The Golden Bear a little while longer and talk excitedly. But soon, they all go away.
"Oh, just a moment," Justus stops Josy. "We would like to examine the other victims' houses a little more thoroughly[5]. Could you show them to us quickly?"
"Sorry," Josy answers, "I really don't have time right now. But ask Mayor Black! If he means what he said last night in The Golden Bear, he will probably[6] help you."
Josy is right. Because of the dramatic events, the mayor is even grateful[7] that someone is taking the initiative[8]. "Why don't you come in right now?" he says and leads them into his house. "Sorry, but we're just renovating[9]." He points to the furniture, the buckets of paint[10]

---

1 once bitten, twice shy: gebranntes Kind scheut das Feuer (wörtlich: einmal gebissen, doppelt schüchtern)
2 to recover: sich erholen
3 paramedic: Sanitäter
4 ambulance: Krankenwagen
5 thoroughly: gründlich
6 probably: wahrscheinlich
7 grateful: dankbar
8 to take the initiative: die Initiative ergreifen
9 to renovate: renovieren
10 buckets of paint: Farbeimer

and the rolls of wallpaper[1] in the corridor. "So, you want to see the houses and rooms in which it happened, right?"
The Three Investigators nod.
"Good. As you may already know, I was the first victim. That was about two months ago."
"Where exactly did the vampire –," Bob hesitates[2] for a moment, "where did it happen?"
"Upstairs, in my bedroom," answers Black and goes ahead. "But I'm afraid there's nothing much left to see[3]. Of course, we cleaned everything up." The mayor goes up the stairs.
"Did your bedroom look more or less like Mary Stamper's just now?" asks Justus.
"Definitely," answers the mayor. "Perhaps even a little more bloody." He opens a door to his right. "In here!"
The three boys go into the room and look round curiously[4]. It is cold and smells of moth balls[5]. And garlic and moth balls are hanging everywhere.
"May we?" Bob asks and points into the room.
"Of course." The mayor nods.
While Justus and Bob start to examine the bedroom thoroughly, Peter is interested in something else.
"Mr. Black," he begins, "did you notice the vampire at all[6]?"
Black shakes his head. "Nothing, absolutely nothing! I read for a long time, as always, drank a little wine, and went to bed. And then I woke up in my own blood."
"Ah yes," Peter nods. "And why are you still here in Yonderwood? Aren't you scared?"

---

1 rolls of wallpaper: Tapetenrollen
2 to hesitate: zögern
3 nothing much left to see: nicht mehr viel zu sehen
4 curiously: neugierig
5 moth balls: Mottenkugeln
6 Did you notice the vampire at all?: Haben Sie irgendetwas vom Vampir mitbekommen?

The mayor shakes his head and then says in a dignified voice[1]: "I am the mayor here, it is my duty[2] to stay until the end, like the captain of a ship. And as long as I stay in rooms like this at night, I am safe."
"At least safe from a vampire," Justus whispers to Bob. The two boys look at each other knowingly[3] and then inspect the room further. Peter joins them. But they don't discover anything strange or unusual.
"There's nothing here that will give us any clues," says Justus after about a quarter of an hour.
"At least we haven't found anything. May we still see the other houses?"
"Certainly!" answers Black and then adds, "You know, I would give everything to have this spook end at last."
"We'll do what we can," Justus tells him.
"Yes," says Black. "Yes, thanks."

The house in which Mrs. Davenport was attacked by the vampire is a little further down the street. Exactly opposite, there is an imposing statue[4] of a lion, which Black proudly[5] points out. "That is a sculpture by Alexandru Zelea, the founder[6] of our small village. He was a highly gifted artist[7]"
The Three Investigators just nod. Not even Justus has heard of an artist with that name, and that says a lot. But the First Investigator is surprised for a moment that a man with such a foreign sounding[8] name has founded a village in California.

---

1 in a dignified voice: mit würdevoller Stimme
2 duty: Pflicht
3 knowingly: *hier* – vielsagend
4 imposing statue: imposante Statue
5 proudly: stolz
6 founder: Gründer
7 a highly gifted artist: ein äußerst begabter Künstler
8 foreign sounding: fremd(ländisch) klingend

There are also no signs of a break in[1] at Mrs. Davenport's house. The door is shut and the windows are undamaged[2]. But on the first floor, Bob notices something.

"Guys!" he calls to his friends. "Take a look here!" the Third Investigator points to four dents[3] in the carpet.

"Hm." Justus examines the cupboard[4] only a few inches[5] away. "The cupboard seems to have stood over there until a short while ago," he guesses and points to the dents. "The chest of drawers[6] has also been moved."

Peter finds some scratches[7] on the floor in front of a small cupboard on the other side of the room. "Also, some of the boards are a bit loose. I can even lift them." Peter shakes a few boards, which creak[8] alarmingly. In the next room, the furniture has also been moved. In the attic[9] some of the roof panels[10] are damaged[11] and the desk has a broken lock.

When The Three Investigators examine Patricia Hamilton's house shortly afterwards[12], they find similar clues. Here too, objects have been moved around not long ago. Some nails are loose and there are signs of damage.

"Strange!" says Justus when they are back on the street. He turns to Black, thoughtfully, "Did the two ladies live alone?"

"Yes."

---

1 break in: Einbruch
2 undamaged: unbeschädigt
3 dent: Einbuchtung, Delle
4 cupboard: Schrank
5 inch: Zoll, angloamerikanische Längeneinheit (1 inch = 2,45 cm)
6 chest of drawers: Kommode
7 scratch: Kratzer
8 to creak: knarren, quietschen
9 attic: Dachgeschoss, Dachboden
10 roof panels: Dachpaneele
11 damaged: beschädigt
12 shortly afterwards: kurz darauf

"And do you think that they normally repaired[1] or changed a lot of things in the house themselves[2]?"

The mayor shakes his head. "I can't imagine that. They are both over 70 and not that strong."

Detective Question

What could be the reason that furniture was moved and some things were damaged in two of the victims' houses?

---

1 to repair: reparieren
2 themselves: *hier* – selbst

9. Beyond the Woods[1]

The Three Investigators have a lot to do the rest of the day. Peter will visit Mrs. Davenport and Mrs. Hamilton. Bob is going to find out everything about Yonderwood and Justus wants to find out more about the rest of the villagers and their backgrounds[2].

It is almost five p.m. when the three boys meet again at their office in Rocky Beach, an old trailer[3] in the yard of *Titus Jonas' Salvage Yard*.

"So, I'm rather curious," says Justus while Peter sinks into an old armchair. "Who is going to begin?"

"Not me," says Bob, who is looking strangely serious. Without another word, he gets a coke from the fridge and leans against the filing cabinet[4].

"Oh … well," answers Justus, a little surprised, "then it's your turn, number two! What did you find out?"

"My charm," begins Peter and smiles, "was once again effective, even though both ladies didn't want to discuss the matter[5] with me at first. They were scared that the vampire would take revenge[6]. After a while they told me more, but that didn't really help either[7]. Neither of them can remember the vampire at all. Mrs. Davenport's memory stopped shortly after she got the prize the evening before in The Golden Bear, and Mrs. Hamilton's black-out started after she held a birthday party for half the village. And as for their houses: Both say their furniture hasn't been moved for a long time."

---
1 beyond the woods: jenseits der Wälder
2 background: Hintergrund
3 trailer: Campinganhänger, Campingwagen
4 filing cabinet: Aktenschrank
5 the matter: *hier* – die Sache, die Angelegenheit
6 would take revenge: sich rächen würde
7 didn't help either: half auch nicht

Justus nods. "I have only one explanation for that. Someone looked around thoroughly after the two ladies moved out."

Peter looks thoughtful. "A burglar[1]? But the houses were not damaged on the outside."

Justus shakes his head. "I think it's much more interesting that after the vampire had driven the ladies from their homes[2], someone was inside them."

"You mean there's a connection[3]?" asks Bob and then answers his own question. "Yes, that's possible."

"If we could take a look at one or two of the other empty houses we would know more," Peter says.

Justus nods. "We have to check that out. As for my results[4], I think I now know why the residents who are still in Yonderwood won't or can't leave."

He checks his notepad. "We know about Josy and her grandmother," he goes on. "Old Black has also told us his reason. Miles doesn't feel like working and lives off his father's money. They simply can't get him out of the house, he just lives from day to day."

"I also found him a bit of a wimp[5]," comments Peter.

"Let's continue – Sylvester Pound, who is an actor and was in a number of horror films and Stamper have the same reason for still being here. Both invested[6] their money in their Yonderwood homes and can't sell them anymore. And both really need the money from the sale."

"And Mary is scared to go out into the wide world alone, right?" Peter guesses.

---

1 burglar: Einbrecher
2 had driven the ladies from their homes: hatte die Damen aus ihren Häusern vertrieben
3 connection: Verbindung, Zusammenhang
4 as for my results: was meine Ergebnisse betrifft
5 wimp: Weichei, Memme, Waschlappen
6 to invest: investieren

"Correct. Josy thinks she's a good person, but a bit helpless and timid[1]. She will probably stay with her father for the rest of her life. By the way, he raised her himself[2]. Her mother died at her birth." Justus turns over the next page of his notepad. "The remaining people are Diesel, the Pastor, and Kowalski. It's clear that Pastor Clark cannot leave his flock[3] alone at this difficult time. And as for Klara Kowalski, Josy thinks she is a little crazy, but harmless. She is part of some magic circle and is sure that Yonderwood has a special aura."

"Oh, a kind of medium[4]," Peter guesses. "Perhaps she made contact with the vampire."

Justus groans[5]. "Peter! Vampires don't exist!"

"I wouldn't be so sure about that[6]," Bob suddenly says.

Justus and Peter spin around.

"What?"

"Bob?"

The Third Investigator bites his lip. "This is what I discovered: Yonderwood was actually founded in the year 1871 by a Romanian immigrant, a stonemason[7] named Alexandru Zelea. He thought there was gold here, but apart from[8] a few nuggets[9] nothing was ever found. However, something else is interesting – the unusual name of the place. Yonderwood can be translated as *beyond the woods*. If, however, one translates *beyond the woods* into Latin, then it results in the word," Bob pauses[10] for a moment and then says, "Transylvania! And that, as we all know, is the home of Count Dracula."

1 timid: schüchtern, ängstlich
2 he raised her himself: er hat sie selber groß gezogen
3 flock: (Schaf)herde
4 medium: Medium, Geisterbeschwörer
5 to groan: stöhnen
6 I wouldn't be so sure about that: da wäre ich mir nicht so sicher
7 stonemason: Steinmetz
8 apart from: außer
9 nugget: Goldklumpen
10 to pause: innehalten

Detective Question

What are the Latin words for wood/forest (Wald) and beyond/on the other side of (jenseits von)?

You will have to find a Latin dictionary to answer this question, you could try to find one on the internet.

10. Night of Horror

"Count Dracula?" Peter says, horrified. "Oh no! So that's the explanation! Probably they killed his wife, or his children, or Zelea himself. And because this guy is a descendant[1] of Dracula he is now avenging himself on[2] the people of Yonderwood!"

"Calm down, Peter!" Justus tells Peter. "Dracula is only a figure in horror literature. There was once a Walachian[3] lord called Vlad Tepes The Impaler[4] because he impaled his enemies with stakes[5]..."

"It's getting better and better!" groans Peter.

"... and this lord at the time was also known by the name of *Dracula* but that ..."

"You see! That's who I mean," Peter interrupts Justus again. "Dracula existed and his great, great whatever grandson is this Zelea! And he's haunting[6] Yonderwood now!"

For a moment or two, Justus is silent. All these strange new connections give him a lot to think about.

"Well, OK," he finally says. "Why don't we go back to Yonderwood and watch the village again tonight. But tomorrow we'll try to find out as much as possible about the place's past. Perhaps the solution[7] to the puzzle really lies in the past."

Peter is not happy. They want to catch a real vampire? At night! In his time! In his element! However, the Second Investigator also knows that this is what they have to do. They can't leave the villagers without trying to help them. However, by sunset, when they reach Yonderwood, he is feeling very scared.

---

1 descendant: Nachfahre
2 he is avenging himself on: er rächt sich an
3 Walachian: walachisch (die Walachei liegt in Rumänien)
4 impaler: Pfähler
5 he impaled his enemies with stakes: er spießte seine Feinde auf Pfähle
6 to haunt: herumgeistern, heimsuchen
7 solution: Lösung

Bob parks his VW-beetle behind the McDonaghough's house. The three boys get out, get their things from the car and, just like the evening before, Justus hands out[1] the walkie-talkies. Then Bob leaves to start the first watch. But nothing happens. No vampire climbs up the wall of the house, no bat lands on the roof and no normal human being disturbs the residents from their sleep. Bob leaves his post at midnight and goes to wake up Justus.

"Justus, wake up!" he whispers when he arrives in the attic. Gently he shakes him awake in his sleeping bag.

"Yes, yes alright," Justus says sleepily, opens up the sleeping bag then puts on his shoes, takes his jacket and walks along the corridor. When he shuts the door, Bob is already falling asleep[2].

"Man, it's cold!" murmurs Justus and starts to shiver.

He thinks for a second and then runs to the old barn[3] next to Homer Diesel's home. But nothing happens during Justus' watch either. Only once, at about two in the morning, the light in Diesel's house goes on. And that's only because, judging by the sound[4], he has to go to the toilet. At three a.m. the First Investigator finally leaves the barn. It's his turn to wake Peter.

The Second Investigator is awake at once. "Did you see him?"

"No, it's your turn."

Peter swallows his rising fear[5] and goes downstairs in his socks. On the way, he decides exactly where he wants to go. Diagonally opposite[6] the McDonaghough's house stands the village church with its small cemetery[7], and on the other side of the field of graves[8] there's

---

1 to hand out: *hier* – verteilen
2 to fall asleep: einschlafen
3 barn: Scheune
4 judging by the sound: dem Klang nach zu urteilen
5 swallows his rising fear: schluckt die steigende Angst herunter
6 diagonally opposite: schräg gegenüber
7 cemetery: Friedhof
8 grave: Grab

a huge[1] water tower. An iron ladder[2] leads to the top from where he can see half the village. But on this evening it's impossible to see much. It is nearly full moon, so the night should be pretty bright[3], but the weather isn't cooperating[4]. Every now and then, big clouds drift[5] across the sky, covering the moon, leaving the village in complete darkness. When the clouds move away, the moonlight shines for a bit until the next clouds arrive, and everything is dark again.

"Well that's great," Peter complains to himself. "How can I be careful if I can't see?"

He pulls his jacket closer and stares out into the darkness. Nothing happens for about half an hour. It's completely still. But suddenly Peter hears something. He can only hear the noise for a very short time. It's a scraping[6] noise. Shortly after that, there is absolute silence again.

The Second Investigator kneels down[7] so he can hear better. A thick black cloud has just hidden[8] the moon again so that he can only see the outlines[9] of the houses. Otherwise it is dark – completely dark.

"Probably a cat," Peter tells himself, trying to pluck up courage[10]. "Or a raccoon[11]."

He listens again. For the next five minutes, nothing happens. Then he hears something again. There is a scraping and someone is groaning!

---

1 huge: riesig
2 iron ladder: eiserne Leiter
3 should be pretty bright: sollten eigentlich recht hell sein
4 to cooperate: kooperieren, mitspielen
5 to drift across the sky: über den Himmel ziehen
6 scraping: schabend
7 to kneel down: sich niederknien
8 hidden: versteckt, verdeckt
9 outline: Umriss
10 to pluck up courage: den Mut zusammennehmen
11 raccoon: Waschbär

Peter flinches[1]. Where is the sound coming from? Where? Feeling scared, he looks around. He puts the walkie-talkie to his mouth, presses the talk button – and at that moment the clouds move away from the moon! Pale silver[2] moonlight illuminates[3] the whole village, the stone lion and Peter, who is sitting up on his water tower. And then it shines on the church tower.

And there it stands! In the window of the church tower! Upright[4], threatening[5], almost majestic[6], a huge man-sized bat spreads its mighty wings[7] and takes off into the night sky! Without a sound, it glides downwards. Only a quiet humming[8] can be heard. Peter stares at it, he can't move. The bat sails right across the village street, spreads out its wings and lands a few yards away from a house. It's the McDonaghough's house!

Darkness! Abruptly it has become dark again. Peter takes a minute to recover from the shock. Then he pulls out the walkie-talkie, pushes the talk button and shouts into it, "The vampire's in the house! He's with you!" And without waiting for an answer, he rushes[9] down the ladder and runs across the dark street towards the McDonaghough's house.

Detective Question

What is strange about the fact[10] that the vampire is in the church tower?

---

1 to flinch: zusammenzucken
2 pale silver: blass silbern
3 to illuminate: beleuchten
4 upright: aufrecht
5 threatening: bedrohlich
6 majestic: majestätisch
7 spreads its mighty wings: breitet seine mächtigen Flügel aus
8 humming: Summen, Surren
9 to rush: eilen
10 fact: Tatsache

11. The Year of Revenge[1]

"First Investigator? Bob?" Peter runs into the room. "Are you hurt? How are you?"
"What's the matter?"
Justus and Bob have got up. They tried to talk to Peter on the walkie-talkie for the last minute, but all they could hear was the sound of someone breathing fast and quick footsteps[2].
"What's the matter?"
"You're OK?"
"Yes, why?" Bob looks at Peter in alarm.
"He's here! The vampire!"
Peter spins around as Josy comes in.
"Why are you making so much noise? It's four in the morning!"
"I've seen the vampire! He's an enormous bat!" Peter shouts. "He flew from the church tower and landed right in front of your house!"
"He flew down from the church tower?" asks Bob doubtfully[3].
"Yes, really! I really can't believe it yet! He stood at the top and took off just like that[4]!"
Justus immediately knows what to do. "Come on! Get the people out of their beds. Bring the flashlights[5]. We have to see if someone is missing[6]!"
However, their search leads to no result, all the villagers come at once and no one is missing.

---

1 revenge: Rache
2 footsteps: Schritte
3 doubtfully: zweifelnd
4 just like that: einfach so
5 flashlight: Taschenlampe
6 to be missing: fehlen

Now, even Jonathan Black is angry. "It's none of us. Can't you finally see that! There are other powers at work here!"
The others nod and agree with the mayor. Only Diesel is silent. A short inspection of the church tower and the landing place in front of the McDonaghough's house doesn't lead to anything. There is only a large shop window, a ring to which dogs can be tied during shopping and an old bike stand[1].
"We'll continue tomorrow," Justus says tiredly and then corrects himself, "I mean, later."
The boys decide to go to Rocky Beach immediately so they can sleep in their own beds for the rest of the night.

They only get back to Yonderwood in the early evening. When they arrive at the McDonaghough's kitchen, Josy and her grandmother are already having dinner.
"And now?" Josy looks at them and asks, "What are you going to do next?"
Justus says, "As long as it's still daylight, we'll look at the church tower properly. Oh, and do you know someone who is well-informed about your village's past? Perhaps something is being kept secret which would shed light on[2] what is happening."
"Pastor Clark," Josy answers. "He knows a lot about Yonderwood."
"Ah, that's great!" Justus says. "We'll ask him to tell us a bit about Yonderwood's past. And then he can show us the tower."
"And we mustn't forget to search[3] a few more houses carefully," Peter reminds them.
Josy looks from one to the other, surprised. "Why? Do you have a clue?"

---

1 bike stand: Fahrradständer
2 which would shed light on: *hier* – das etwas erhellen/aufklären würde
3 search: *hier* – durchsuchen

Justus quickly tells her what they have discovered in Mrs. Davenport's and Mrs. Hamilton's houses and what conclusions they have reached[1].

"Hm," Josy comments. "But you didn't notice anything like that at the Blacks'?"

Justus looks at her wide-eyed[2]. "No! – Now you mention it! That's right! We didn't notice anything there, did we, guys?"

Peter and Bob shake their heads.

"And Mary was only bitten the night before last," Josy murmurs to herself.

Bob whistles appreciatively[3]. "Hats off! You would be a first class investigator!"

"Justus," Bob turns to his friend, "Josy is right. We should also search the Stamper's house. Even if we were on guard last night."

"We'll do that."

The three boys get up and help Josy clear the table before going on their way.

"Go to the church via[4] the cemetery," Josy tells them. "Then you'll pass the Pastor's house."

"OK!" Justus says.

Then they say goodbye, quickly walk to the Pastor's house and ring the doorbell. Pastor Clark opens the door a few moments later.

"My young friends," he says. "Welcome. What brings you here?"

"Good evening! After the events of this morning, we would like to look at the inside of the church," Justus says. "Josy told us that you know a lot about Yonderwood's history."

"That's right," Pastor Clark smiles.

---

1 to reach conclusions: Schlüsse ziehen
2 wide-eyed: mit großen Augen
3 whistles appreciatively: pfeifft anerkennend
4 via: *hier* – durch

"Now," Justus continues, "we wonder if there's anything in Yonderwood's history that might shed light on all those strange happenings."

Pastor Clark shakes his head slowly and looks worried.

"I thought about that too, my son. God's will is unfathomable[1]. However, all our residents were good Christians."

"But let's go to the church. On the way there I'll tell you the highlights[2] of Yonderwood's past."

During the following half hour, The Three Investigators hear about all the good things the people in Yonderwood did over the last hundred years.

Pastor Clark stops at almost every second grave, talks without stopping and then leads the boys to the old part of the cemetery. The Three Investigators become more and more tired from listening. But they haven't gone more than ten steps, when Bob suddenly stops and points to an old tombstone.

"Is this really the grave of *the* Ken Hanson, I mean *the* burglar king who is better known by the name of 'Ken the Cat'? Because the dates of his birth and death are about right[3]."

Pastor Clark looks displeased[4]. "Yes, the unhappy creature[5] lies here."

"He lived here?" Naturally, Justus also knows about the famous burglar.

"He was not only buried[6] here, he spent the last two days of his life in Yonderwood."

They can see that the Pastor does not want to talk about the subject[7].

---

1 God's will is unfathomable: Gottes Wille ist unergründlich
2 highlight: Höhepunkt
3 to be about right: in ungefähr stimmen
4 displeased: unerfreut
5 creature: Wesen, Kreatur
6 buried: begraben
7 subject: *hier* – Thema

Peter asks, "Isn't there a rumour[1] that throughout his life he piled up[2] lots of money which was never found?"

"Maybe," Pastor Clark answers. "Come, let's go on. There's still a lot here to see."

Reluctantly[3] the boys move away from the burglar's grave; however, the real surprise is still to come. They have arrived at the furthest corner of the cemetery and Peter notices it first.

"The ... tombstone," he stammers[4] and points to the ground. "It's been moved quite a bit! The grave is ... open."

"What?" Pastor Clark calls out in a horrified voice and spins around. They are standing in front of a grave which is obviously very old. There is no tombstone and the grave itself is not covered with earth but with a heavy stone slab[5] which is very worn[6] and most of it is hidden by moss[7]. But the slab has been moved! There is a gaping crack[8] at least half a yard[9] wide.

"The tomb[10] has been opened!" Pastor Clark grows pale[11]. "The vampire has risen[12] from this grave."

"The vampire? Has risen from this grave?" Bob is horrified.

"That's it," says Pastor Clark. "That's God's punishment[13]! The Lord is punishing us for our sins[14]!"

---

1 rumour: Gerücht
2 to pile up: anhäufen
3 reluctantly: widerwillig
4 to stammer: stottern
5 stone slab: Steinplatte
6 worn: *hier* – verwittert
7 moss: Moos
8 gaping crack: klaffender Spalt
9 yard: angloamerikanische Maßeinheit, 1 yard = 0.91 Meter
10 tomb: Grab, Grabkammer
11 to grow pale: blass werden
12 to rise: aufstehen, aufsteigen
13 punishment: Strafe
14 to punish someone for his sins: jemanden für seine Sünden bestrafen

Meanwhile, Justus kneels down and tries to read the inscription[1] on the slab.

"It's Zelea's grave," he says slowly, "Alexandru Zelea is buried here. And when I look at this slab, I don't believe it moved on its own. Someone helped. It's much too heavy! And something else is strange. Judging by the inscription, Zelea died exactly one hundred years ago!"

"Exactly one hundred years ago?" asks Bob in surprise.

"Yes, that's why it seems even clearer to me that it's not a coincidence[2]."

"You mean," Peter looks at Justus, "that Zelea waited exactly a hundred years to avenge himself on[3] Yonderwood? That this is his year of revenge?"

Justus gets up again. "I won't disagree with you that it might be a year of revenge, Second Investigator. But maybe we can find out more if we open the grave and see who is or is not inside."

"You want to open the grave?" Peter shouts.

Justus nods. "If you permit[4], Pastor Clark."

The Pastor closes his eyes. "You are right, my son. We have to confront[5] this evil."

While Pastor Clark begins to pray, The Three Investigators push the enormous slab to the side with all their strength. In the grave they find a big wooden coffin.

"That's open, too!" Bob calls out. "Look, the lid[6] is on crooked[7]."

"Somehow, I'm not surprised," Justus comments and climbs into the grave. Then he pushes the coffin's lid to one side.

---

1 inscription: Inschrift
2 coincidence: Zufall
3 to avenge himself on: um sich an ... zu rächen
4 if you permit: wenn Sie es erlauben
5 to confront sthg./someone: sich etwas/jemandem stellen
6 lid: Deckel
7 crooked: schief

Up above, Bob and Peter hold their breath[1] while Pastor Clark prays loudly.

"No vampire!" says Justus, as he looks inside the coffin. "This is a completely normal skeleton."

"But what's this?" He kneels down and picks up something from the coffin.

"What have you got there?" Peter asks impatiently[2] and he and Bob stare into the grave.

"Come on, tell us!"

Justus gives a small shining metal object[3] to his friend. It's a bullet[4]!

"It looks," he says thoughtfully, "as if Zelea did not die a natural death."

Detective Question

Why might Zelea want to[5] avenge himself on the residents of Yonderwood?

---

1 to hold one's breath: den Atem anhalten
2 impatiently: ungeduldig
3 small shining metal object: ein kleiner, glänzender Metallgegenstand
4 bullet: Kugel
5 might want to: will vielleicht

12. Searching for Clues

Pastor Clark suddenly finds it all too much. "I have to inform my brothers and sisters about this," he whispers. "One thing is sure. We have sinned and will be punished. So if you can do without me now, I would be grateful. God protect[1] you, my young friends. God protect us all!" Then he leaves.

Peter helps Justus out of the grave. "Then it must be as I thought, Zelea was killed, and exactly one hundred years ago!"

Justus stands next to the grave and looks at the bullet, thinking.

"And now," Peter continues, "thanks to his vampire blood, he comes out of his grave and takes revenge on every Yonderwood resident for some strange reason."

Justus continues[2] to stare at the bullet. "Yes, hm. I have to examine this at Headquarters.[3]"

"What do you want to examine?" asks Bob.

"Are you listening to me at all?" Peter shakes his head.

"The bullet," answers Justus. "And yes, Peter, I am listening. But I don't reply to[4] every bit of nonsense."

"That's not nonsense!"

"And why?" Bob points to the bullet.

"I'll tell you when I've been to Headquarters." Justus puts away the bullet. "And now we'll all take a look at the church!"

"Oh great!" Peter complains. "And is anybody going to talk to me?"

---

1 to protect: beschützen
2 to continue to do sthg: fortfahren, etwas zu tun
3 headquarters: Zentrale
4 reply (to sthg): (auf etwas) antworten

It is cold and rather dusty[1] in the church. On the left of the altar, a wooden staircase leads to the pulpit[2] and behind the altar at the side is the entrance to the vestry[3].

"That probably leads up to the tower," Bob whispers and points to another door on the right.

"Good, then we'll go up," Justus answers.

They go through the wooden door and climb up the stairs to the church tower. The old stairway is extremely steep[4].

"That's at least thirty yards," Bob gasps and looks up.

"You're probably ... right," Justus says, he is sweating.

A few minutes later, Peter steps through the door first.

"What happened here?" he says, surprised.

All over the room, there are wooden beams[5] and boards[6], as well as all kinds of carpentry tools[7]. The floor is covered in sawdust[8].

"They are repairing the wooden structures," says Bob, pointing up.

There, next to the giant bells[9] they see some new beams. The Three Investigators start looking around. They search the whole room, hoping to find clues. But they find nothing informative. It is only when Justus leans out of the western window that he notices something interesting.

"Look, guys!" he shouts. "Look at that!"

Peter and Bob run to him.

"Do you mean the steel hook[10]?" Peter says and points to a huge hook above the window.

---

1 rather dusty: ziemlich staubig
2 pulpit: Kanzel
3 vestry: Sakristei
4 steep: steil
5 beam: Balken
6 board: Brett
7 carpentry tools: Schreinerwerkzeug
8 sawdust: Sägemehl, Sägespäne
9 bell: Glocke
10 steel hook: Stahlhaken

"Probably for the motor winch¹," Bob guesses. "They have to get the boards upstairs somehow."

"It's used for that, too," Justus answers mysteriously and looks down into the street.

"What are you thinking?" asks Peter.

Justus points to his watch. "I'll explain it to you downstairs. Now let's get out of here. The bells will start to ring in a minute and it will be hellishly² loud."

The boys leave the room and hurry downstairs. Halfway down, the bells start to ring. Even in the tower, the noise is still deafening³. The Three Investigators run faster.

"Made it⁴!" Justus shouts as he sprints⁵ out of the tower.

Out of breath⁶, he stops in front of the entrance.

"Are you alright?" jokes Peter.

"Shut up⁷," answers Justus while the bells above him slowly stop ringing.

"It's good that we got out of there in time," Bob says. "Otherwise I would be deaf⁸ by now."

He breathes out and – stops short.

"Well?"

He looks more closely at the floor in front of him and then to the right in the direction of the altar room. Confused, he says, "There is sawdust lying around here, too."

"Of course," Justus answers. "The workers have to get down from the tower and then they come through here."

---

1 motor winch: Motorwinde
2 hellishly: höllisch
3 deafening: ohrenbetäubend
4 (I've) made it: (ich hab es) geschafft
5 to sprint: sprinten
6 out of breath: außer Atem
7 Shut up!: Halt die Klappe!, Halt's Maul! (umgangssprachlich)
8 deaf: taub

"No, take a look!" Bob replies. "The trail[1] doesn't lead to the exit, it leads *inside,* into the church! The workers don't go in to pray straight after[2] work when they are still dirty."

Justus answers, "That really is strange, Third Investigator."

Like bloodhounds[3], noses to the ground, the three boys follow the trail of sawdust. At a distance of one or sometimes two big steps apart, a few crumbs[4] of the sawdust lie on the ground.

"Looks more and more as if the sawdust fell out of the sole[5] of someone's shoe while he was walking," Peter guesses.

"The clue leads directly to the altar room," says Justus.

The Three Investigators walk to the front of the church and up the steps to the altar room. But the trail ends abruptly in front of the altar.

"Ah," Peter wonders, "And now? Where did he go, whoever it is?"

"Perhaps the soles were clean by the time he got here?" Bob guesses.

"I don't think so." Justus points to the last heap they found. "Here there are still a lot of crumbs. I would be surprised if those are the last crumbs that fell out."

Peter sits down on the floor and then leans his back against the altar. It is a little uncomfortable because the front[6] of the altar is decorated with a relief[7] with various[8] faces and symbols, but he still finds a place to lean on.

"Then perhaps he went back the same way," he says. "He came up to here, stood still, turned around and … " in the middle of the sentence, the Second Investigator makes a surprised sound. Something

---

1 trail: Spur
2 straight after: direct nach
3 bloodhound: Bluthund, Spürhund
4 crumb: Krümel
5 sole: (Schuh)Sole
6 the front: die Vorderseite
7 relief: Relief
8 various: verschiedene

has given way[1] behind him and in the next second they hear a grinding[2] sound. Peter jumps up, spins around and together with Justus and Bob he watches as the whole altar slowly slides[3] backwards.

Detective Question

What is strange about the trail of sawdust that The Three Investigators find?

---

1 something has given way: etwas hat nachgegeben
2 grinding: knirschend
3 to slide: rutschen, gleiten

13. The Vampire's Crypt[1]

"What's that?" Peter shouts. "What's happening?"
"You must have set off[2] a secret mechanism[3]," Justus replies.
Suddenly the altar stops moving. It comes to a stop after about a yard and reveals[4] a staircase going down. From the entrance, stale[5] air comes up to The Three Investigators.
"That's … that's the entrance to the crypt under the church," Peter says.
Justus examines the altar more closely. "The crypt is probably just as secret as the mechanism which opens it."
The First Investigator touches several of the stone animal heads at the front of the altar. When he touches a bull[6], the altar slides forward again into its original position.
"Aha, now we've got it!"
He sets off the mechanism a second time and the altar slowly slides back again.
Bob examines the first step of the entrance. "The trail really leads down there," he says quietly. "There is more sawdust lying on the first and third step, on the left side."
Justus raises his eyebrows, "Only on the left side? Interesting."
Then he takes three big white candles from the altar and gives two to the other investigators.
"Well then, let's see what has led our mystery man down there."
Unwillingly[7], Peter lights the candles.
"I don't feel good about this, guys."

1 crypt: Gruft
2 to set off: *hier* – in Gang setzen, aktivieren
3 secret mechanism: geheimer Mechanismus
4 to reveal: offenbaren
5 stale: abgestanden
6 bull: Bulle, Stier
7 unwillingly: widerwillig

The candles light up¹ the darkness here and there while the boys climb down the stairs. There are bare walls left and right and darkness below².

"It's pretty big," Bob whispers, when they reach the end of the staircase.

A large underground vault³ lies in front of them. Slowly the boys feel their way. But they arrive at the end of the vault without coming across anything unusual.

"OK. Now to the right and then back to the entrance," decides Justus.

The Three Investigators turn to the right and then walk along the back wall for a bit. When they have almost come to the end of the left wall, something appears in the flickering⁴ light of the candles.

"A coffin!" They cry out together.

"A ... big coffin!" whispers Peter. "The vampire's coffin! Here ... he sleeps during the day."

"Nonsense!" says Justus and quickly walks towards the coffin.

It is a plain black wooden coffin, without decorations or any inscriptions. It just lies there.

The First Investigator grabs⁵ the lid of the coffin. "Help me, guys! Let's look inside!"

Bob grabs the middle of the coffin's lid while Peter takes the bottom end and together they lift⁶ the lid. The Second Investigator shuts⁷ his eyes. He doesn't want to see what is inside. And Bob, too, avoids⁸ looking inside the coffin. Only Justus has a look inside.

"Well, look at that!" he says. "What do we have here?"

"Is it ... him?" Peter asks.

---

1 to light up: erhellen
2 below: unten
3 vault: Gewölbe
4 flickering: flackernd
5 to grab: hier – greifen
6 to lift: heben
7 to shut: schließen
8 to avoid doing something: es vermeiden, etwas zu tun

"No, the master of the house[1] is not in, if that's what you mean," says Justus. "But he left a few things here."
"Things? What things?" Peter opens his left eye.
"A rope[2] and a zip wire trolley[3] for example," Justus answers.
"If you use them properly, you can glide from here to there easily, – if you know what I mean."
"The hook," Bob remembers.
"And probably the ring you can tie dogs to," Justus adds. He puts his hand into the coffin and takes out three yellowing pieces of paper.
"And here we have … Bible verses," he murmurs in surprise.
"Bible verses?" Peter asks in disbelief[4].
"Revelations 1.15, Chronicles 4.11 and …," Justus looks at the last note in his hand, "… 2 Solomon 3.8." He reads the verses. "Something is underlined[5] in each of the verses. Waterfall. House of God. Dog's Head. And on the bottom of every piece of paper there are some initials: R.D., F.H. and X.N."
"A vampire who collects[6] Bible verses?" Peter is completely confused.
"Guys! I've found some sleeping pills! And a thick syringe![7]" Bob holds up a red and white medicine box and a big empty needle[8].
Justus nods. "Things are starting to become clearer."
"I don't understand it."
Peter is now feeling brave[9] enough to have a look inside the coffin. "But this is …!"

---

1 master of the house: Herr des Hauses
2 rope: Seil
3 zip wire trolley: Rollengleiter
4 in disbelief: ungläubig
5 underlined: unterstrichen
6 to collect: sammeln
7 syringe: Kanüle
8 needle: *hier* – Spritze
9 brave: mutig

He unfolds an enormous black piece of material which turns out to be[1] a brilliant costume[2]!
"The costume of a huge bat! Then ... this was ..."
"... the batman which you saw in the night," Justus finishes his sentence.
"So it was a cape[3]!" Bob feels the soft material. "Unbelievable – and there's something else in here." Peter gives the cape to Bob.
"A book!" The Second Investigator lifts a thin old book out of the coffin and opens it. "The diary[4] of a Xavier Noir."
"What?"
Justus looks at one of his Bible verses, "X.N."
"What does it mean?" Peter asks excitedly.
"Hm."
Peter moves closer to the candles. "It's difficult to read. But here, wait, 17.4.1881. I think it says 'Ken is putting the town into a state of terror and fright.' And here, 18.4.1881. Thank God, Ken is dead. Today he just fell -"
Peter stops. A cold wind blows through the crypt and the candles begin to flicker[5]. "Why is there suddenly wind in here?"
Justus turns around. "That can only happen if someone comes into the church."
"Then let's get out of here![6]" Bob shouts.
"If it's the wrong person, we're caught in a trap[7]!"
At that moment, another strong gust of wind[8] blows through the crypt and blows out one of the candles. And then they hear a grinding sound.

1	which turns out to be ...: dass sich als ... entpuppt
2	costume: Kostüm, Verkleidung
3	cape: Umhang, Cape
4	diary: Tagebuch
5	the candles begin to flicker: die Kerzen beginnen zu flackern
6	Let's get out of here!: Lasst uns hier verschwinden!
7	to be caught in a trap: in einer Falle gefangen sein
8	gust of wind: Windstoß

"Damn!" Peter swears.
"The altar! It's closing!"
The boys run to the exit.
"Faster," Bob shouts. "Faster!"
But just as Peter rushes around the corner they hear mocking[1] laughter. It comes from above, where the gap is only open a hand's width[2]. Peter stops in horror. Unable to move, he sees the opening narrow to a thin slit[3]. Then the horrible laughter dies down and, with a thud[4], the huge altar stone closes the opening to the crypt.

Detective Question

How did the 'vampire' manage to make it look as if he was flying?

---

1 mocking: höhnisch
2 a hand's width: eine Handbreite
3 narrow to a thin slit: sich zu einem schmalen Schlitz verengen
4 thud: dumpfer Schlag

14. No Time!

Peter stops dead.[1] "He's buried[2] us alive! He wants us to die here!"
"Oh God!" Bob bursts out.
Justus looks thoughtful. "This draught[3]," the First Investigator murmurs. "The only way we could feel it in the crypt ... "
"... is if there is another exit somewhere else!" Peter completes the sentence. "Of course! Boss, you're a genius!"
"I don't know if it's an exit, but there must be some connection to the outside."
After some searching, they discover the wall where the draught came from.
"That could be the connection," Justus shines the candle on a heap of rocks, bricks[4] and earth. "There probably was an earthquake[5]. But we have to clear a way[6] for ourselves."
The boys start at once. As there is not enough space for all three of them, only two at a time can clear away the rubble[7]. While Peter and Bob start, Justus gets the diary out of the coffin and by the light of the candle, he tries to read in it. The work continues slowly. It is becoming clearer that they have found a way out. But The Three Investigators have to work with their hands. And the rocks are often so big and heavy that the boys have to use all their strength to make the opening bigger, inch by inch. Hour after hour passes. The Three Investigators groan and sweat. They take turns again and again while one of them reads the diary. It is almost midnight when Justus takes a break again. He sits down on the floor and reads the next page.

1 to stop dead: wie angewurzelt stehen bleiben
2 to bury: begraben
3 draught, BrE (draft, AmE): Luftzug
4 brick: Backstein
5 earthquake: Erdbeben
6 to clear a way: *hier* – einen Weg freiräumen
7 rubble: Schutt

After a few minutes he suddenly says, "Unbelievable!" and quickly turns another page. "That's … I can't believe it!"

At this moment Peter comes out of the tunnel. "We've got through! We've done it!" he calls.

Bob is behind him. Justus jumps up.

"Quick! Let's take the things from the coffin and then get back to the cemetery at once[1]!"

"The cemetery!" say Peter and Bob. "What's happening?"

"There's no time now for explanations. We have to hurry!"

Peter and Bob ask no more questions. They sense[2] that something is very wrong. The boys pack up the things they found in the coffin and squeeze through[3] the tunnel and into the open. They come out next to the cemetery wall.

"Absolutely right," Justus whispers and holds his candle up high. "And now look for the grave of a man called Hank, who was at least thirty years old in 1881."

"What? I don't understand. You want us to … "

"Not now," Justus interrupts, "every minute counts!"

Justus sends Peter and Bob in different directions and then starts to look himself. After five minutes, Bob comes running towards Justus. "Over there lies a Hank. He was forty-four years old in 1881. He was called McDonaghough. Perhaps Eleonora's great granddad?"

"My God," Justus says.

At the same moment, the church bells begin to ring, it is midnight.

"We have to go to the McDonaghough's at once!"

The three boys run towards the house. From a distance[4], they can already see that the door to the McDonaghough's house is wide open!

"I hope we are not too late!" Justus gasps.

---

1 at once: sofort
2 sense: spüren
3 to squeeze through sthg.: sich durch etwas durchzwängen
4 from a distance: *hier* – von Weitem

They split up[1] and search the rooms. But just as the Third Investigator is about to turn on the light in the kitchen, a dark figure runs into him, pushes past him and rushes down the stairs.

"Hey!" Bob stumbles backwards. He steadies himself[2], lets the cape fall to the ground and runs after the figure. "He's here! Over there!"

Bob runs down the stairs along the corridor, sprints outside and sees the figure vanish around the corner of the house. He sprints as fast as he can around the corner. But suddenly a black shadow[3] appears[4] in front of him. He can only get out a low sound before he is hit by a fist[5]. While the Third Investigator falls to the ground, someone runs away. Justus and Peter find him fifteen seconds later.

"Follow that guy, I'll take care of Bob," says Justus and kneels down on the floor next to his friend.

Peter nods and runs off.

"Bob? Is everything OK?"

The Third Investigator groans and puts his hand up to his right eye.

"Oh man, I'm sure I'll get a black eye[6]."

"Did you recognize anyone?"

"A black shadow, very quick, hits really hard. Do you know the guy?"

Justus has to laugh. "Come, get up, I'll help you."

Peter returns. "Gone. He's vanished into thin air[7]."

Justus nods, "Then let's find the McDonaghoughs. I hope nothing's happened to them."

---

1 to split up: sich trennen
2 he steadies himself: er fängt sich, er erlangt sein Gleichgewicht wieder
3 shadow: Schatten
4 to appear: erscheinen
5 fist: Faust
6 black eye: blaues Auge
7 to vanish into thin air: sich in Luft auflösen

They find both of them in their rooms. Josy and her grandmother have been gagged[1] and tied to their beds[2]. The old lady is obviously not well and stares into space. After The Three Investigators free her, Josy says, "The bastard!" She sits on the bed next to her grandmother and rubs her painful wrists[3].

"Did you see who it was?" Bob gives Josy a glass of water.

"No, he didn't turn the light on."

"And what did he want?" Peter gives Josy a worried look.

"No idea. After he tied us up, he searched the whole house with a flashlight at least for an hour. Then I heard you."

"And you found him in the kitchen, did you say?" Justus asks Bob.

"Yes."

"Hm." Justus gets up. "I have to check something."

He goes over into the kitchen and Peter and Bob follow him. The First Investigator turns on the light and looks around. But after just a few seconds he finds what he is looking for.

"I thought so!"

He goes to the kitchen table and picks up something from the table. It seems to be a small framed picture. Justus turns it around so that Peter and Bob can see it too.

"The Bible verse?" both call out.

"Yes, the Bible verse."

Detective Question

How does Justus know that there is a connection to the outside from the crypt?

---

1 they have been gagged: sie wurden geknebelt
2 tied to their beds: an ihre Betten gefesselt
3 painful wrists: schmerzende Handgelenke

15. The Cat's Treasure

"And what does all this mean?" Peter doesn't understand a thing.
Justus sits down. "I can't explain that to you right now. If we act[1] quickly then we can still catch the guy."
He puts his head in his hands and concentrates hard.
"Waterfall, House of God, dog's head," he mumbles. "As Daniel was not guilty, he was snatched from the lion's jaws. Waterfall, House of God, dog's head. As Daniel – lion! Yes. Lion! Bob! Where's our map?" he suddenly calls out.
Bob thinks for a moment, "It must be upstairs."
Justus jumps up. "Come on, let's go."
The First Investigator runs up the stairs. Peter and Bob sprint after him. In the small attic, Justus searches through Bob's rucksack and pulls out a pencil and a map. He quickly opens the map on the floor.
"I'm looking for the rock where Peter banged his head a few days ago. Where did that happen?"
"The one that looked like a dog's head?" Bob asks, pointing at a spot on the map. "It must have been here."
"And there towards the west is the waterfall." Justus points to a thin blue line on the map. Then his finger moves along the map to a building in Yonderwood, which is marked by a cross[2].
"The church, the House of God." Then the First Investigator grows even more excited.
"And where do you think the lion is?"
"The one by Zelea?"
"Yes."

---

1 act: handeln
2 marked by a cross: durch ein Kreuz gekennzeichnet

Peter uses his finger to trace[1] along Yonderwood's main street.
"Just about there," he says.
"That's what I think, too."
Justus connects the different places with straight lines and then draws a circle around the point where the lines cross[2]. "And that's where we have to go."
"But why, Justus?" Peter is bursting with curiosity[3].
"I'll explain it on the way there. But now, let's go."
In the next three minutes, Bob and Peter find out what Justus read in the diary.
The story is so unbelievable that the two boys would like to stop right there so that they can find out more. But Justus tells them to hurry.

Outside the village lies a flat plane[4] covered with big rocks. There are a few tall trees here and there – mostly[5] oak[6] trees.
Justus points ahead. "Look at the tree trunk[7]. The big spot two yards above the ground could be a hole."
"It is a hole in the trunk!" Peter whispers as they stand under the oak tree. "OK, help me up and I'll see what's inside it."
Justus takes Bob's hands and they both bend[8] their knees a little bit. Peter puts his right foot onto their clasped[9] hands and pushes himself up with his left.
Using his hands, he climbs up the trunk.
Justus and Bob straighten up so that Peter's face is now exactly in front of the hole.

---

1 to trace: *hier* – entlangfahren
2 to cross: sich (über)kreuzen
3 to burst with curiosity: vor Neugier platzen
4 plane: Ebene
5 mostly: meist, vor allem
6 oak: Eiche
7 trunk: (Baum)stamm
8 bend their knees a little bit: beugen die Knie ein wenig
9 clasped: verschränkt

He reaches into the hole with his right hand. "There's nothing."
"Are you sure?"
Peter searches in the hole in the trunk.
"The hole isn't that big and there is definitely … wait!"
"Have you found anything?" Bob's voice shakes with excitement[1].
"Yes! A … bag. Right at the back. Made of leather."
"That must be it," gasps Justus.
His hands hurt, but he doesn't want to give up now.
"I'll have it in a minute," Peter gasps. "It's really heavy. Now! I have it! Let me down!"
Justus and Bob lower Peter down[2].
"Let's see! What's inside?"
All of a sudden, there is a click behind them.
The three of them spin round and freeze[3].
A dark figure is waving a pistol at them[4].
His face is masked by a cloth[5] – the kind bank robbers used to wear – that covers all of his face except his eyes.
Justus clears his throat.
"We won't give you this treasure," he says, trying to make his voice sound firm[6].
"Are you crazy?" whispers Peter.
The stranger growls and waves his pistol even more.
Justus grabs the bag. "I can imagine … "
A shot rings through the night and hits the tree trunk just above the heads of The Three Investigators.
"We understand," Peter takes the sack and throws it at the figure's feet. "There you are."

---

1 to shake with excitement: vor Aufregung zittern
2 to lower (down): herunterlassen
3 to freeze: *hier* – erstarren
4 is waving a pistol at them: fuchtelt mit einer Pistole herum, die auf sie gerichtet ist
5 cloth: *hier* – ein Tuch
6 to make his voice sound firm: seine Stimme fest klingen lassen

The stranger picks up the sack in one hand. He moves away, step by step, his pistol still pointed at[1] the three of them.

When he is far away enough, he turns around and runs in the direction of Yonderwood.

"We should have first checked who wasn't at home in bed in Yonderwood," grumbles Bob.

"That would have been less dangerous[2]."

"But I didn't want this guy to take the treasure for himself and then hide it so it would be impossible to find again," Justus replies and adds, "Anyway, now I know how we can catch the fellow."

Detective Question

What was the purpose (*Zweck*) of the Bible verses?

---

1 his pistol still pointed at them: seine Pistole immer noch auf sie gerichtet
2 that would have been less dangerous: das wäre weniger gefährlich gewesen

16. Experiments

The next evening, The Three Investigators ask Josy to bring together the residents of Yonderwood in The Golden Bear again.
Justus and Bob wait for them in the inn, while[1] Peter decides to turn up[2] later. As the residents arrive, they look at the two investigators suspiciously, because Josy hasn't told anyone what is going on. And when Justus and Bob say that they want to solve[3] the mystery of Yonderwood, the suspicion grows stronger. However, after they have finished their report[4], the mood[5] changes abruptly.
"What is this you are telling us?" Homer Diesel jumps up. "The burglar's loot[6] was hidden in a tree for a hundred and twenty years? And the entire spook was because of that?"
"So, about a hundred and twenty years ago, this Ken the Cat died in our village," Pound says. "Then the priest and four men found a bag full of gold that was worth a fortune[7]."
"But no-one knew who the owner of the stuff was," Stamper adds. "They asked around, investigated, but everyone shouted, 'This is mine.' So nobody was sure. After that, the priest decided to take care of the money until the real owner was found."
"But five years later, he was on his deathbed[8]," Jonathan Black continues. "And no-one knew whose gold it was. Then the priest hid the money in a safe place. He gave each of the four men who were with him at the time a tip in the form of a Bible verse. But only all four

---

1 while: während
2 to turn up: auftauchen
3 solve: lösen
4 report: Bericht
5 mood: Stimmung
6 loot: Beute
7 worth a fortune: ein Vermögen wert
8 he was on his deathbed: er lag im Sterben

verses together gave away[1] the hiding place, so no-one could go on their own."

"But surely they could have divided the gold among themselves?" asks Klara Kowalski.

Justus shakes his head.

"According to the diary[2] there was never any danger of that. The men were all absolutely reliable[3]. The priest simply wanted to make sure that nobody would be led into temptation[4]."

"Good. Carry on," says Miles. "In the verses, four places were mentioned. The church, the lion, the waterfall and the dog's head. And if you connect these, you come to the oak tree where you found the treasure."

Pastor Clark clears his throat. "Do I understand the connection between this story and the vampire correctly? Someone found this diary and found out where he had to look for the Biblical verses. Then he pretended to be a vampire because he wanted to drive away the residents. That way, he could search for the Bible verses in their houses."

"Exactly," Justus nods.

"He used the fact that the village was founded by a Romanian who came from the same region as Count Dracula and also named this place after that region ... Yonderwood. And to make the spook more believable, he came up with a few details which I must admit are very clever. Apart from doing the 'vampire's attacks' he also appeared now and again as an enormous bat and used Zelea's tomb as an explanation for the vampire's actions ... revenge."

"And Zelea did not die a hundred years ago?" asks Pound.

"No, he died a hundred and six years ago. The numbers on the tombstone were changed. Zelea wasn't really shot, the bullet in the coffin

---

1 to give away: *hier* – Aufschluss geben über
2 according to the diary: dem Tagebuch zufolge
3 reliable: verlässlich
4 to be led into temptation: in Versuchung geführt werden

was brand new and came from a modern weapon. Someone probably just put it into the coffin, but more about that later."

Diesel says, "But we didn't know anything about these connections until Pastor Clark informed us yesterday."

"But that wasn't necessary, because the connections had to come to light[1] sooner or later to explain these happenings. It was only a matter of time," answers Bob. "It was all planned carefully."

"Please show me the syringe again," Miles asks Bob.

The Third Investigator passes it to him.

"So with that he caused the victim's wounds. And all the blood was from a pig or a cow?"

"That is what we think," Bob nods.

"And the victims didn't notice because he gave them a strong sleeping pill. With Mrs. Davenport, he used the celebration here in The Golden Bear, with Mrs. Hamilton, her birthday and with Mary probably the lemonade. After that, he waited till midnight to finish his work. With Mary he first had to move the garlic and the crosses, otherwise no-one would have believed in the vampire anymore."

"And now," Justus smiles, "we would like to unmask[2] the vampire by doing a small experiment[3]."

For two seconds there is a surprised silence. Everyone stares at Justus, but then complete chaos breaks out. Everyone talks at once, jumps up and looks at one another.

"You mean the culprit[4] is among us?" Jonathan Black asks excitedly.

"Impossible! Quite impossible!" Pastor Clark calls out.

"Never," Miles dismisses the idea[5].

But Justus and Bob stay completely calm.

---

1 had to come to light: mussten ans Licht kommen
2 unmask: enttarnen
3 by doing a small experiment: indem wir ein kleines Experiment machen
4 culprit: Schuldiger
5 to dismiss the idea: den Gedanken verwerfen

They put a can[1] in the middle of the room and Justus says, "We want every one of you – one after the other – to kick the can towards the exit." Everyone looks puzzled and all conversation stops.
"You want us to do what?" Pound asks disbelievingly[2].
"Please, just kick," replies Justus.
The residents hesitate.
"What is this nonsense?" Diesel protests.
"Please!"
Pastor Clark steps forward. He positions himself, lifts his cassock[3] and kicks the can towards the black curtain in front of the entrance door.
"Like this?"
Justus smiles.
"Thanks, many thanks. Next please."
Miles goes next, then Pound, then Mrs. Kowalski who needs two attempts[4] because she misses[5] the first time, then Diesel shoots, though he is looking very grumpy[6]. While this is happening, Peter comes in. He is carrying his rucksack and nods to his friends. When everyone has finished, Justus looks at Peter and Bob for a moment. He goes over to the can and slowly picks it up. Everybody is watching him expectantly[7].
Then Peter suddenly calls out, "Miles" and Bob, "Mr. Pound". Miles Black and Sylvester Pound spin around and at that moment Peter and Bob throw each of them a tennis ball[8]. The yellow balls fly towards both of them. Pound lifts his right hand and grabs the ball out of the air and Miles' left hand shoots forward to catch the ball.

1	can: (Konserven)Dose
2	disbelievingly: ungläubig
3	cassock: Talar, Soutane (Priestergewand)
4	attempt: Versuch
5	to miss : *hier* – verfehlen, danebenschießen
6	grumpy: mürrisch, schlecht gelaunt
7	expectantly: erwartungsvoll
8	throw each of them a tennis ball: werfen jedem von ihnen einen Tennisball zu

Miles looks angry. "What's that supposed to mean?" he asks.

"Yes. What was that?" Pound wants to know.

"That," says Justus, "was further[1] proof that," he hesitates briefly, "you, Miles, are our man. You're behind everything!"

Detective Question

Why do you think The Three Investigators make everyone kick a can and also throw balls at Black and Pound?

---

1   further proof: ein weiterer Beweis

17. The Real Scoundrel[1]

Miles gasps. "Are you crazy?"
"This is going too far," protests old Black.
"Give us a few minutes, then we'll explain everything," Justus continues unimpressed[2].
Looking hostile, the residents stare at the three of them.
No-one believes them. Only Josy smiles at them.
"We already told you," Justus begins, "how we found the trail that led to the tomb. As we said, the scoundrel probably left it the evening before, after he took the rope down from the church tower."
"We found the sawdust on every second step on the left side of the stairs going down into the crypt. People nearly always climbs stairs with their strong foot first, whether they are going up or down. The trail starts on the first step on the left. That proves we are looking for a left-footer and our little experiment has just shown that you, Miles, are one."
Miles grins condescendingly.[3] "That's great."
"But Mr. Pound is also a left-footer," Peter continues.
"But you are left-handed too, as we just saw when you caught the ball."
"And as my black eye is on the right," Bob points at his black eye, "a left-handed person must have given it to me. And also, the scoundrel who threatened us[4] near the oak tree held the weapon in his left hand."
Miles Black snorts. "There are a million left-footed and left-handed people."

---

1 scoundrel: Schurke
2 unimpressed: unbeeindruckt
3 condescendingly: herablassend
4 to threaten someone: jemanden bedrohen

He looks around as if he is expecting[1] applause.
But now some of the residents are looking very thoughtful.
"Right," Justus says, still friendly. "However, there was one victim whose house strangely[2] wasn't damaged."
Justus pauses. "Jonathan Black."
"Miles, you didn't have to get anybody to leave your home. You didn't have to search for anything either, because you already found what started all this: the diary of your ancestor[3]."
The First Investigator looks at Miles challengingly[4]. "You found it in your house during the renovation."
The villagers don't say a word, but Miles starts laughing loudly. However, the laughter sounds fake[5].
"And I bit my father, did I?" he asks in amusement.
Peter shrugs, "Yes, because that was the easiest way to start the vampire spook."
Thoughtfully, Pastor Clark asks, "What did you mean just now by ancestor?"
Justus opens the first page of the diary.
"There," he points to the writing. "This is the diary of a certain Xavier Noir. He was probably of French origin[6] and as there are no more Noirs anymore in Yonderwood and as the last trace[7] of the Noirs disappeared at the cemetery about ninety years ago, it seems that the Noirs changed their name to fit their new home."
"If you translate 'noir' into English," Bob takes over, "you get 'black'."
"Black!" hisses Klara Kowalski.

---

1 to expect: erwarten
2 strangely: *hier* – merkwürdigerweise
3 ancestor: Vorfahre
4 challengingly: herausfordernd
5 fake: unecht
6 of French origin: (von) französischer Herkunft
7 trace: Spur

The residents start murmuring and whispering excitedly. Suspicious looks are thrown at Miles Black. But he is still looking relaxed and almost bored and orders another beer from Stamper.

"That really is a fantastic story which you have invented[1]."

He shakes his head, "But nobody will believe this nonsense. I am supposed to[2] go round as a vampire in order to get hold of[3] a treasure? You must be dreaming."

Justus nods to Peter.

"Oh yes, about the treasure. There is another thing," Peter says ironically and takes the rucksack off his shoulders.

"As the lock picker of our investigator team I had a look around your house during this meeting. I am sorry, but unusual situations sometimes require special measures[4]."

Miles jumps up, "You did what? That's burglary[5]!"

His father stays seated. It is clear from the look on his face that he is scared of further revelations[6].

"And obviously you underestimate[7] us greatly. That only you or your father could be the culprit was clear to us from the facts mentioned[8]. And because you are left-handed and left-footed, obviously all the suspicion falls on you. And the final proof is in what I found when I looked under the mattress."

Peter takes the same leather bag out of his rucksack which he had taken out of the hole in the tree. He holds it up triumphantly, "Ken the Cat's treasure!" Now there is complete chaos.

---

1 to invent: erfinden
2 I am supposed to: *hier* – ich soll angeblich
3 in order to get hold of a treasure: um an einen Schatz zu kommen
4 to require special measures: besondere Maßnahmen erfordern
5 burglary: Einbruch
6 revelation: Offenbarung
7 to underestimate: unterschätzen
8 the facts mentioned: die erwähnten Fakten

Mrs. Kowalski shrieks[1] – Pastor Clark crosses himself[2] and starts to pray, Diesel and Pound jump up, Stamper shouts, "You dog!" And even Eleonora starts to scold[3] loudly.

Only Josy and old Black are quiet. Josy because she already knew everything and Jonathan Black because he is so ashamed[4]. But before anyone can do anything, Miles suddenly gets up and pulls his pistol. Everybody stops dead.

"You are not that clever after all, are you?" Miles sneers[5]. "You remember the pistol, don't you?" he smiles.

"He brought the pistol!" Peter gasps.

"Yes I have, you smartass[6]! Come on, give me the bag."

Suddenly a spark lights up in Justus' eyes and Bob and Peter relax a bit, too.

"I bet the bullet from Zelea's coffin is from this gun. Am I right?" The First Investigator smiles.

Miles looks confused. "That … that can't matter to you[7] now."

"And I would just like to say that regarding the treasure[8] everything is clear now."

Even though Miles is moving closer to him, Justus stays surprisingly cool. "Ken sold off the loot after various burglaries and bought himself gold coins with the profits. He obviously wanted to retire[9] because the police had come dangerously close."

"What are you blathering[10] on about? Come, give me the bag. I'm not going to say it again."

1 to shriek: kreischen
2 crosses himself: bekreuzigt sich
3 to scold: schimpfen
4 ashamed: beschämt
5 to sneer: spotten
6 smartass: Schlaumeier, Besserwisser (umgangssprachlich)
7 to matter to someone: jemandem etwas ausmachen
8 regarding the treasure: was den Schatz betrifft
9 retire: sich zur Ruhe setzen
10 to blather: schwafeln

Miles is getting more and more angry.

"Ah, I have another question," Peter says. "Do you believe in all this vampire nonsense?"

Miles is shocked. "That's enough!" he growls and points his pistol at[1] the Second Investigator. "I'm going to count to three and then shoot. One ..."

"Miles!" – Josy jumps up – "Stop that! You can't do that!"

"Two!"

A garlic bulb[2] flies through the air and lands far away from the investigators in a corner of the restaurant. Miles turns around and instinctively[3] points the pistol in that direction.

"Three," calls Stamper from behind him and hits him over the head with one of the crosses, using all his strength.

Miles immediately sinks to the floor, unconscious. The pistol falls out of his hand.

"That was for Mary, you rat!" The landlord shouts and hangs the cross up again.

Everyone in the room breathes a sigh of relief[4]. Diesel slaps Stamper on the shoulder[5] and Justus takes the gun. Jonathan Black is a nervous wreck[6]. He kneels down on the floor next to his son looking unhappily at all of them.

"Forgive me," he says quietly. "I'm so sorry."

"You see!" Peter gives Justus a playful punch in the side[7]. "The old horror stories are true after all!"

The First Investigator looks at his friend, confused. "I'm afraid I don't understand."

---

1 points his pistol at: richtet seine Pistole auf
2 garlic bulb: Knoblauchknolle
3 instinctively: instinktiv
4 to breathe a sigh of relief: einen Seufzer der Erleichterung ausstoßen
5 to slap someone on the shoulder: jemandem auf die Schulter klopfen
6 to be a nervous wreck: fertig mit den Nerven sein
7 to give someone a playful punch: jemandem spielerisch einen Hieb versetzen

"Well, garlic and crosses," says Peter cheerfully. "They *do* help fight vampires – you only need to know how."
Justus rolls his eyes, "Oh Peter."

Detective Question

Why was Jonathan Black one of the 'vampire's' victims?

Englisch-Deutsche Wortliste

a lot of – *viel, eine Menge*
act – *handeln*
agree – *zustimmen*
alarming – *beunruhigend*
ambulance – *Krankenwagen*
ancestor – *Vorfahre*
apart from that – *außerdem*
appear – *erscheinen*
ashamed – *beschämt*
at least – *mindestens*
at once – *sofort*
attempt – *Versuch*
attic – *Dachgeschoss, Dachboden*
authentic – *authentisch*
avenge oneself on – *sich an … rächen*
avoid doing something – *es vermeiden, etwas zu tun*
backfire – *nach hinten losgehen*
background – *Hintergrund*
bare rocks – *nackte Felsen*
barn – *Scheune*
be a nervous wreck – *fertig mit den Nerven sein*
beam – *Balken*
beg for forgiveness – *um Vergebung betteln, um Verzeihung bitten*
bell – *Glocke*
below – *unter, unten*
beyond the woods – *jenseits der Wälder*
bike stand – *Fahrradständer*
black eye – *blaues Auge*

blather – *schwafeln*
blinds – *Rolladen, Jalousien*
blood-curdling – *markerschütternd*
bloodhound – *Bluthund, Spürhund*
board – *Brett*
bolt of lightning – *Blitz*
bon viveur – *französisch für: Lebenskünstler*
borrow – *(sich) ausleihen*
boxer – *Boxer (Hunderasse)*
brave – *mutig*
break in – *Einbruch*
break open – *aufbrechen*
brick – *Backstein*
brook – *Bach*
buckets of paint – *Farbeimer*
bull – *Bulle, Stier*
bullet – *Kugel*
burglar – *Einbrecher*
burglary – *Einbruch*
buried – *begraben*
burst out – *herausplatzen*
burst with curiosity – *vor Neugier platzen*
bury – *begraben*
business card – *Visitenkarte*
butcher – *Metzger*
can – *(Konserven)Dose*
cape – *Umhang, Cape*
carpentry tools – *Schreinerwerkzeug*
cassock – *Talar, Soutane (Priestergewand)*
caught in a trap – *in einer Falle gefangen*
cemetery – *Friedhof*

chain – Kette
challengingly – herausfordernd
change one's mind – die Meinung ändern
chest of drawers – Kommode
clasped – verschränkt, umklammert
clear the table – den Tisch abräumen
clear up the matter – die Angelegenheit (auf)klären
clear one's throat – sich räuspern
cliff – Klippe
climb – klettern
cloth – Tuch, Stoff
clue – Anhaltspunkt, Hinweis
coffin – Sarg
coincidence – Zufall
collapse – zusammenbrechen
collar – Kragen
collect – sammeln
comment – bemerken, kommentieren
common sense – gesunder Menschenverstand
complain – sich beschweren
concussion – Gehirnerschütterung
condescendingly – herablassend
confront – konfrontieren
confused – verwirrt
connection – Verbindung, Zusammenhang
continue to do something – fortfahren, etwas zu tun
convince – überzeugen
cooperate – kooperieren, mitspielen
costume – Kostüm, Verkleidung
cover – bedecken
covered in blood – blutüberströmt

crawl on all fours – *auf allen Vieren krabbeln*
creak – *knarren, quietschen*
creature – *Wesen, Kreatur*
creepy – *unheimlich*
crooked – *schief*
cross – *sich (über)kreuzen*
crumb – *Krümel*
crypt – *Gruft*
culprit – *Schuldiger*
cupboard – *Schrank*
curiously (adv) – *neugierig*
curtain – *Vorhang*
cute – *süß*
damaged – *beschädigt*
damned – *verdammt*
deaf – *taub*
deafening – *ohrenbetäubend*
décor – *Dekor, Einrichtung*
delicate – *zart, empfindlich*
dent – *Einbuchtung, Delle*
descendant – *Nachfahre*
deserted – *verlassen*
detective office – *Detektivbüro*
diagonally opposite – *schräg gegenüber*
diary – *Tagebuch*
die down – *verstummen*
disbelievingly – *ungläubig*
discover – *entdecken*
displeased – *unerfreut*
disturbed – *beunruhigt*
door handle – *Türklinke*

doubtfully – *zweifelnd*
draught, BrE **(draft,** AmE**)** – *Luftzug*
drown – *ertrinken*
drugstore – *Drogerie*
dump – *Dreckloch, Müllhalde*
dust – *Staub*
duty – *Pflicht*
earthquake – *Erdbeben*
embarrassing – *peinlich*
encouragingly – *aufmunternd, ermutigend*
entrance – *Eingang*
event – *Ereignis*
examine – *untersuchen*
exceptionally – *außerordentlich*
expect – *erwarten*
expectantly – *erwartungsvoll*
experience – *Erfahrung*
fact – *Tatsache*
fake – *unecht*
fall asleep – *einschlafen*
fellow residents – *Mitbewohner*
fight – *Streit*
filing cabinet – *Aktenschrank*
fist – *Faust*
flash – *blitzen*
flashlight – *Taschenlampe*
flickering – *flackernd*
flinch – *zusammenzucken*
flock – *(Schaf)herde*
floor – *Stockwerk*
footsteps – *Schritte*

for ages – seit Ewigkeiten
foreign sounding – fremd(ländisch) klingend
forgive – verzeihen
founder – Gründer
freeze – erstarren
from a distance – von Weitem
further proof – weiterer Beweis
gap – Lücke
garlic – Knoblauch
garlic bulb – Knoblauchknolle
gas stove – Gaskocher, Gasherd
gathered (to be) – versammelt (sein)
gently – sanft, leise
ghost town – Geisterstadt
glare – wütend anstarren
grab – 1. packen 2. greifen
grateful (adj) – dankbar
gratefully (adv) – dankbar
grave – Grab
grinding – knirschend
groan – ächzen, stöhnen
grow pale – blass werden
grumble – murren
grumpy – mürrisch, schlecht gelaunt
gust of wind – Windstoß
guys – Jungs, Leute
hair net – Haarnetz
hair pins – Haarnadeln
hallway – Flur, Diele
hand out – verteilen
haunt – herumgeistern, heimsuchen

headquarters – *Zentrale*
heartthrob – *Schwarm*
hellishly – *höllisch*
helpless – *hilflos*
hesitate – *zögern*
hidden – *versteckt, verdeckt*
highlight – *Höhepunkt*
hiss – *zischen*
horrified – *entsetzt*
hostile – *feindselig*
howl – *heulen*
huge – *riesig*
humming – *Summen, Surren*
hunter – *Jäger*
illuminate – *beleuchten*
impaler – *Pfähler*
impatiently – *ungeduldig*
in a dignified voice – *mit würdevoller Stimme*
in a forced way – *gezwungen*
in case – *falls; für den Fall, dass*
indecisive – *unentschlossen*
inn – *Gaststätte*
innkeeper – *Wirt*
inscription – *Inschrift*
insulated mat – *Isomatte*
intently – *aufmerksam, gespannt*
interrupt – *unterbrechen*
intrude – *sich aufdrängen*
invent – *erfinden*
invest – *investieren*
investigator – *Ermittler*

iron ladder – *eiserne Leiter*
irritable – *gereizt*
kind – *freundlich, liebenswürdig*
kneel down – *sich niederknien*
lid – *Deckel*
lift – *heben*
light up – *erhellen, beleuchten*
lock picker – *Schlossknacker*
locked – *abgeschlossen*
lockpick – *Dietrich*
lonely – *einsam*
loot – *Beute*
lower (down) – *herunterlassen*
majestic – *majestätisch*
mantelpiece – *Kaminsims*
mark – *Mal, Spur*
master of the house – *Herr des Hauses*
matter – *Sache, Angelegenheit*
matter to someone – *jemandem etwas ausmachen*
mayor – *Bürgermeister*
medium – *Medium, Geisterbeschwörer*
middle-aged – *mittleren Alters*
miss – *verfehlen, danebenschießen*
missing – *fehlend*
mix up – *durcheinanderbringen*
mocking – *höhnisch*
mood – *Stimmung*
moss – *Moos*
mostly – *meist, vor allem*
moth balls – *Mottenkugeln*
motor winch – *Motorwinde*

murmur – *murmeln*
myth – *Mythos*
needle – *1. Nadel, 2. Spritze*
nightgown – *Nachthemd*
nonsense – *Unsinn*
notice – *bemerken*
nugget – *Goldklumpen*
oak – *Eiche*
obviously – *offensichtlich*
occupant – *Bewohner*
once bitten, twice shy – *gebranntes Kind scheut das Feuer (wörtlich: einmal gebissen, doppelt schüchtern)*
one by one – *einer nach dem anderen*
order – *befehlen*
out of breath – *außer Atem*
outline – *Umriss*
own – *besitzen*
pale – *blass*
paramedic – *Sanitäter*
pause – *innehalten*
peel – *abblättern*
pile up – *anhäufen*
pillow – *Kissen*
pitiful – *erbärmlich, bemitleidenswert*
plane – *Ebene*
pour – *1. sich ergießen 2. strömen*
pretend – *so tun als ob*
probably – *wahrscheinlich*
protect – *beschützen*
proudly – *stolz*
pulpit – *Kanzel*

puncture – *Einstich*
punishment – *Strafe*
raccoon – *Waschbär*
raise – *heben*
rather – *ziemlich*
rattle – *1. rütteln 2. verunsichern*
reach conclusions – *Schlüsse ziehen*
realize – *erkennen, einsehen*
recognize – *wiedererkennen*
recover – *sich erholen*
rectangle – *Rechteck*
regular – *regelmäßig*
reliable – *verlässlich*
relief – *Relief*
relieved – *erleichtert*
reluctantly – *widerwillig*
renovate – *renovieren*
repair – *reparieren*
reply (to sthg) – *(auf etwas) antworten*
report – *Bericht*
require special measures – *besondere Maßnahmen erfordern*
reserved – *reserviert*
resident – *Einwohner*
responsible – *verantwortlich*
retire – *sich zur Ruhe setzen*
reveal – *offenbaren*
revelation – *Offenbarung*
revenge – *Rache*
rise – *aufstehen, aufsteigen*
roof panels – *Dachpaneele*
rope – *Seil*

rub – *reiben*
rubble – *Schutt*
rumble – *Grollen*
rumour – *Gerücht*
rush – *eilen*
sales counter – *Verkaufstresen*
saved – *gerettet*
sawdust – *Sägemehl, Sägespäne*
scold – *schimpfen*
scoundrel – *Schurke*
scraping – *schabend*
scratch – *Kratzer*
search – *durchsuchen*
seem – *scheinen*
sense – *spüren*
separated – *getrennt*
serious – *ernst*
set off – *in Gang setzen, aktivieren*
setting sun – *untergehende Sonne*
several – *einige*
shadow – *Schatten*
shelter – *Unterschlupf*
shiver – *zittern, schaudern*
shortly afterwards – *kurz darauf*
shriek – *kreischen*
shrug – *mit den Schultern zucken*
shut up – *still sein, das Maul halten (umgangssprachlich)*
shut – *schließen*
shutters – *Fensterläden*
sigh – *seufzen*
skeptical – *skeptisch*

slam – *knallen*
slide – *rutschen, gleiten*
slip – *ausrutschen*
sneer – *spotten*
snort – *schnauben*
sole – *Schuhsole*
solution – *Lösung*
solve – *lösen*
speechless – *sprachlos*
split up – *sich trennen*
spooky – *gruselig*
sprint – *sprinten*
stale – *abgestanden*
stammer – *stottern*
steel hook – *Stahlhaken*
steep – *steil*
stone slab – *Steinplatte*
stonemason – *Steinmetz*
strain – *Anspannung*
strangely – *merkwürdigerweise*
stress – *betonen*
stumble – *stolpern*
subject – *Thema*
suck – *saugen*
superstitious – *abergläubisch*
supposed to be – *angeblich*
suspicion – *Misstrauen, Argwohn*
swear – *fluchen*
syringe – *Kanüle*
take turns – *sich abwechseln*
teapot – *Teekanne*

thoroughly – *gründlich*
thoughtfully – *nachdenklich*
threaten someone – *jemanden bedrohen*
threatening – *bedrohlich*
timid – *schüchtern*
tissue – *(Papier)Taschentuch*
tomb – *Grab, Grabkammer*
tombstone – *Grabstein*
towel – *Handtuch*
trace – *entlangfahren*
trace – *Spur*
trail – *Spur*
trailer – *Campinganhänger, Campingwagen*
tray – *Tablett*
treasure – *Schatz*
(tree)trunk – *Baumstamm*
trouble – *bekümmern, irritieren*
trust – *vertrauen*
turn up – *auftauchen*
unassuming – *unscheinbar, unauffällig*
unconscious – *bewusstlos*
undamaged – *unbeschädigt*
underestimate – *unterschätzen*
underlined – *unterstrichen*
understanding – *verständnisvoll*
unimpressed – *unbeeindruckt*
unmask – *enttarnen*
unwillingly – *widerwillig*
upright – *aufrecht*
various – *verschiedene*
vault – *Gewölbe*

vestry – *Sakristei*
via – *durch*
victim – *Opfer*
waitress – *Kellnerin*
watch – *Wache*
weird – *merkwürdig, seltsam*
while – *während*
wimp – *Weichei, Memme*
whisper – *flüstern*
worn – *1. abgenutzt, 2. verwittert*
wound – *Wunde*
wring out – *auswringen*
youthful – *jugendlich, jung*
zip wire trolley – *Rollengleiter*

Nützliche Detektiv-Ausdrücke:

Hier sind einige Vokabeln und Redewendungen, die hilfreich sind, wenn man über Verbrechen und Detektivarbeit spricht.

break into a house – *in ein Haus einbrechen*
burglar – *Einbrecher*
burglary – *Einbruch*
case – *Fall*
collect evidence – *Beweismaterial/Hinweise sammeln*
commit a crime – *ein Verbrechen begehen*
criminal – *Kriminelle(r), Verbreche(r)*
culprit – *Schuldige(r)*
detective – *Detektiv*
discover a clue – *einen Hinweis entdecken*
examine – *untersuchen*
evidence – *Beweismaterial*
Freeze! – *Keine Bewegung!*
guilty – *schuldig*
innocent – *unschuldig*
investigate a case – *in einem Fall ermitteln*
investigation – *Ermittlung*
investigator – *ein Ermittler, eine Ermittlerin*
launch an investigation – *eine Ermittlung starten*
look out for something – *auf etwas achten*
lockpick – *Dietrich*
point a gun/pistol at someone – *ein Gewehr/eine Pistole auf jemanden richten*
to pick locks – *Schlösser knacken*

prove that someone is guilty/innocent – *beweisen, dass jemand schuldig/unschuldig ist*
search – *durchsuchen*
solve a case – *einen Fall lösen*
steal something – *etwas stehlen*
suspect – *ein Verdächtiger, eine Verdächtige*
suspicious behaviour – *verdächtiges Verhalten*
suspicious person – *eine verdächtige Person*
thief – *Dieb*
tie someone up – *jemanden fesseln*
weapon – *Waffe*

Übungen

Chapter :

1. Fill in the gaps
Hier ist eine kurze Zusammenfassung mit den wichtigsten Informationen aus dem ersten Kapitel, aber es fehlen ein paar Wörter. Kannst du die fehlenden Wörter einsetzen?

1. Peter has hit his head on a cliff which looks like the head of a _____.

2. He is unhappy because the other two investigators make _____ of him.

3. The Three Investigators are going on a weekend trip because they want to _____ and don't want to solve tricky _____.

4. They decide to walk down to a little village called _____.

5. When they get there, the village is deserted. Peter says it's a _____.

2. Nature vocabulary
Auf ihrer Wanderung sehen die 3 ??? viele Dinge. Streiche durch, was sie nicht sehen.

- a waterfall
- a wolf
- a cliff
- a brook
- a valley
- a lake
- the Pacific ocean
- a river

Chapter 2:

3. The Storm

Hier findest du einige Verben, die man benutzen kann, um Blitz, Donner, Regen und Wind zu beschreiben. Welche Verben passen zu welchem Substantiv? (Es gibt jeweils mehrere Verben, die zu einem Substantiv passen.)

a) lightning
b) thunder
c) rain
d) wind

Tipp!
Wenn du eines der Wörter nicht kennst, kannst du es unter www.pons.eu nachschauen.

to pour down, to blow, to crash, to fall, to rumble, to flash, to strike, to make a bang, to howl

4. What's going on at The Golden Bear?
Wähle die passende Antwort:

1. The Three Investigators go into The Golden Bear to
a) ask for the way.
b) get out of the rain.
c) meet a friend.

2. The Three Investigators find the inn strange because
a) there are garlic and crosses everywhere.
b) there are garlic and tomatoes everywhere.
c) there is a vampire in the inn.

3. The people in the inn
a) greet the boys in a very friendly way.
b) are very drunk and noisy.
c) don't answer Peter's greeting.

Chapter :

5. Fear and confusion in Yonderwood
Die Sätze sind durcheinandergeraten. Kannst du sie wieder in die richtige Reihenfolge bringen?

1. in The Golden Bear/do not like/the atmosphere/the boys
2. a girl called Josy/ring the bell at the drugstore/when/opens the door/the boys
3. the strange happenings/does not want to talk/Josy/about/with the boys/in Yonderwood
4. that/are scared/there is/the people of Yonderwood/a vampire in Yonderwood

Chapter :

6. Vampires!
Welche Beschreibung passt zu welchem Wort? Verbinde!

1. another word for 'scared'   a) shiver
2. you get it when a vampire bites you b) bat
3. vampires like to drink it   c) frightened
4. an animal that flies at night   d) wound
5. you do it when you are cold or scared e) blood

Chapter :

7. Peter and Justus

Der erste und der zweite Detektiv sind sich, was das Übernatürliche angeht, sehr uneinig. Setze das passende Wort in die Lücke!

reason, common sense, superstitious, supernatural, powers

Tipp!
Wenn du ein Wort kennst, kannst du oft den Sinn eines verwandten Wortes erraten. Hier sind drei Beispiele von verwandten Substantiven und Adjektiven:
- superstition *(Aberglaube)*, superstitious *(abergläubisch)*
- reason *(Vernunft)*, reasonable *(vernünftig)*
- powers *(Mächte)*, powerful *(mächtig)*

Manchmal kann ein Wort sogar als Adjektiv und als Substantiv benutzt werden:
- the supernatural *(das Übernatürliche)*, supernatural *(übernatürlich)*

1. Justus believes everything can be explained by _____.
2. He thinks that people who believe in vampires are _____.
3. Peter is afraid that there are dangerous _____ at work in Yonderwood.
4. Peter believes in the _____, Justus doesn't.
5. Justus thinks Peter should use _____.

Chapter :

8. The Residents of Yonderwood
Wer ist wer? Verbinde den Namen mit der passenden Beschreibung!

1. Otis Stamper
2. Mary Stamper
3. Sylvester Pound
4. Homer Diesel
5. Jonathan Black
6. Miles Black
7. Eleonora McDonaghough

8. Pastor Clark
9. Klara Kowalski

a) the minister (*Pfarrer*) in the village
b) the owner of the inn
c) the mayor of Yonderwood
d) he used to be an actor
e) a strangely dressed woman
f) she is waitress in the inn
g) Josy's grandmother who owns the drugstore
h) a *bon viveur*
i) the mayor's son

Chapter :

9. What's wrong?
In der Zusammenfassung der Ereignisse von Kapitel 7 haben sich ein paar kleine Fehler eingeschlichen. Streiche die falschen Informationen.

In the morning, Mary Stamper runs out of the house screaming. Her pyjamas are covered with blood. She collapses on the ground. Pastor Clark carries her back to the house and takes her pulse. The garlic and the crosses have been moved into the bedroom. Justus is surprised that there is so little blood.

Chapter 8:

10. Collecting evidence
Suche das passende Wort aus – oft passt mehr als eins:

1. To find out more, The Three Investigators examine / search / test   the victims' houses.
2. They are hoping to find garlic / clues / evidence .
3. They are looking for anything that is unusual / strange / tasty .
4. In some of the houses, they notice / ignore / hope   that things have been moved and damaged.

Chapter 9:

11. Information
Finde die richtige Antwort:

1. At first Peter does not get much information from the victims because
a) they do not like him.
b) they are not at home.
c) they are scared of the vampire.

2. Otis Stamper does not leave Yonderwood because
a) his wife died there.
b) he cannot sell his house.
c) he loves living there.

3. Peter thinks Klara Kowalski is
a) a vampire hunter.
b) a kind of medium.
c) a very attractive woman.

4. Bob finds out that Yonderwood
a) was founded by a man from Transylvania.
b) means 'inside the woods'.
c) is more than 300 years old.

Chapter :

12. Vampire Crossword

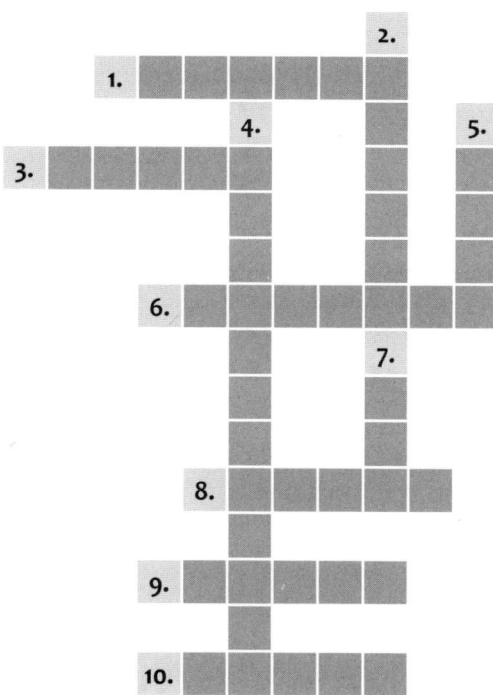

Across:
1. Knoblauch
3. Kreuz
6. Rache
8. Zähne
9. Grab
10. Blut

Down:
2. Sarg
4. übernatürlich
5. beiβen
7. Fledermaus

Chapter :

13. In the cemetery

In diesem Kapitel besuchen die 3 ??? den Friedhof. Hier findest du noch einmal einige wichtige Vokabeln, die alle mit dem Thema Friedhof zu tun haben. Aber die Buchstaben sind durcheinander geraten. Kannst du sie in die richtige Reihenfolge bringen? Zur Hilfe findest du neben jedem Wort einen Tipp.

Tipp!
Oft ist es leichter, Vokabeln, die inhaltlich zusammen gehören, zusammen zu lernen.

1. etceryme — Another word for graveyard.
2. uryb — After someone dies, you _____ him.
3. fifnoc — A box you put dead people in.
4. gevar — A place where a dead person lies.
5. mobtestno — It has the name of the dead person on it.
6. kostelen — The bones of a dead (or living) person.

Chapter :

14. Combine!

1. The church tower is full of sawdust because
2. There is a hook in the wall because
3. The boys leave the tower quickly because
4. The trail of sawdust is strange because

a) the church bells are going to start ringing.
b) the woodwork is being repaired.
c) the workers need it to pull the wood up to the tower.
d) it stops in front of the altar.

Chapter :

15. How good is your memory?
Welche wichtigen Anhaltspunkte finden die 3 ??? im Sarg in der Gruft? Versuche, dich an alle Dinge, die sie finden, zu erinnern und schau erst danach im Kapitel oder in den Lösungen nach.

_____
_____
_____
_____
_____
_____

Chapter :

16. Combine!

In diesem Kapitel findest du einige zusammengesestzte Ausdrücke. Kannst du sie richtig kombinieren? Als Hilfe findest du die deutsche Übersetzung.

1. take
2. hurry
3. tie
4. vanish
5. take a
6. black

a) up
b) eye
c) into thin air
d) turns
e) someone up
f) break

Tipp!
Viele Wörter, die im Deutschen reflexiv sind, also mit ‚sich' benutzt werden, sind es im Englishen nicht. Zum Beispiel sich verbessern = improve – nicht improve yourself! Auch in dieser Übung findest du zwei Ausdrücke, die im Deutschen reflexiv sind, aber im Englischen nicht. Welche sind es?

sich abwechseln, jemanden fesseln, sich in Luft auflösen, sich beeilen, eine Pause machen, blaues Auge

Chapter :

17. Fill the gaps!
Hier ist eine Zusammenfassung der wichtigsten Ereignisse aus Kapitel 15. Aber es fehlen ein paar wichtige Wörter. Kannst du den Text vervollständigen?

1. In the Bible verses, The Three Investigators find clues for four places: a cliff that's shaped like a dog's head, a church, the statue of a lion and a _____.

2. They look up the places on their _____.

3. When they connect the places on the map, they find the place where the _____ is hidden.

4. They find it in a hole in a _____.

5. But then, a stranger comes and points a _____ at them.

6. When Justus does not give him the bag, he _____ at the tree.

7. Peter gives him the bag and he _____ away.

Chapter :

18. Bob's report

In dem Bericht, den Bob über den Vampirfall geschrieben hat, haben sich einige Rechtschreibfehler eingeschlichen – in jedem Satz befindet sich einer. Kannst du sie finden? Wenn du Hilfe brauchst, dann schau dir die korrigierte Version B) an und vergleiche sie mit der fehlerhaften Version A).

A) Ken the Cats treasure was hidden in a tree. After he died, the people in the vilage found the gold. Because they could not find out who the reall owner was, they decided to put it in a safe place. The Bibel verses were clues for the hiding place. Somebody found out about the treasure when he found an old diery. He pretended to be a vampir so that he could search the victims' houses. The blood on the pilows was animal blood.

Tipp!
Oft entstehen Fehler dadurch, dass man vergisst, einen Buchstaben zu verdoppeln oder Buchstaben verdoppelt, wo nur ein Einzelbuchstabe stehen sollte.

B) Ken the Cat's treasure was hidden in a tree. After he died, the people in the village found the gold. Because they could not find out who the real owner was, they decided to put it in a safe place. The Bible verses were clues for the hiding place. Somebody found out about the treasure when he found an old diary. He pretended to be a vampire so that he could search the victims' houses. The blood on the pillows was animal blood.

Chapter :

19. What happens when?
Die Zusammenfassung der Ereignisse des letzten Kapitels ist durcheinander geraten. Bringe die Sätze in die richtige Reihenfolge!

a) Miles pulls out his pistol.

b) Justus explains why Miles must be the 'vampire'.

c) Stamper hits Miles over the head with a cross.

d) Peter takes Ken the Cat's bag out of his rucksack.

e) Someone throws garlic across the room.

f) Peter makes a joke about garlic and vampires.

g) Miles turns towards the place where the garlic has landed.

Lösungen

Chapter 1:

1. Fill in the gaps
1. Peter has hit his head on a cliff which looks like the head of a **dog**.
2. He is unhappy because the other two investigators make **fun** of him.
3. The Three Investigators are going on a weekend trip because they want to **relax** and don't want to solve tricky **cases**.
4. They decide to walk down to a little village called **Yonderwood**.
5. When they get there, the village is deserted. Peter says it's a **ghost town**.

2. Nature vocabulary
a waterfall, ~~a wolf~~, a cliff, a brook, a valley, ~~a lake~~, the Pacific ocean, ~~a river~~

Detective Question 1:
Peter calls Yonderwood a ghost town because there is nobody there.
Verlassene Städte, vor allem alte Goldgräberstädte, werden oft als ‚Geisterstadt' bezeichnet. Außerdem wirkt das Dorf durch den heraufziehenden Sturm noch unheimlicher, so dass der Name besonders passend erscheint.

Chapter 2:

3. The Storm
a) lightning – to flash, to strike
b) thunder – to rumble, to crash, to make a bang
c) rain – to pour down, to fall
d) wind – to blow, to howl

4. What's going on at The Golden Bear?
1b) The Three Investigators go into The Golden Bear to get out of the rain.
2a) The Three Investigators find the inn strange because there are garlic and crosses everywhere.
3c) The people in the inn don't answer Peter's greeting.

Detective Question 2:
The people in the inn are probably scared and don't want anybody to notice that they are there.
Eine weitere mögliche Erklärung ist, dass sie die Fensterläden geschlossen haben, damit niemand durch das Fenster hineinkommen kann.

Chapter 3:

5. Fear and confusion in Yonderwood
1. The boys do not like the atmosphere in The Golden Bear.
2. A girl called Josy opens the door when the boys ring the bell at the drugstore.
   Oder: When the boys ring the bell at the drugstore, a girl called Josy opens the door.
3. Josy does not want to talk about the strange happenings in Yonderwood with the boys.
4. The people of Yonderwood are scared that there is a vampire in Yonderwood.

Detective Question 3:
Josy does not want to talk about the décor in The Golden Bear because she finds the situation embarrassing and scary. *Es ist Josy peinlich, dass all die Dorfbewohner an einen Vampir glauben; gleichzeitig will sie das Thema aber auch vermeiden, weil es ihr Angst macht.*

Chapter 4:
6. Vampires!
1c) frightened, 2d) wound, 3e) blood, 4b) bat, 5a) shiver

Detective Question 4:
If there was a real vampire, he would drink all the blood. *Da der Vampir seine Opfer beißt, um ihr Blut zu trinken, ist es unwahrscheinlich, dass viel Blut verschüttet wird (es sei denn, es handelt sich um einen besonders ungeschickten Vampir).*

Chapter 5:
7. Peter and Justus
1. Justus believes everything can be explained by <u>reason</u>.
2. He thinks that people who believe in vampires are <u>superstitious</u>.
3. Peter is afraid that there are dangerous <u>powers</u> at work in Yonderwood.
4. Peter believes in the <u>supernatural</u>, Justus doesn't.
5. Justus thinks Peter should use <u>common sense</u>.

Detective Question 5:
It's a good idea to find out more about the residents because that way The Three Investigators can find out who has a motive to pretend to be a vampire. *Wenn es sich nicht um einen wirklichen Vampir handelt, sollten die 3 ??? soviel wie möglich über die Dorfbewohner erfahren. Sie können dann feststellen, ob sich irgendjemand ungewöhnlich verhält und ob es ein mögliches Motiv wie Rache oder Geldgier gibt, dem der Spuk dient.*

Chapter 6:
8. The Residents of Yonderwood
1b) Otis Stamper – the owner of the inn
2f) Mary Stamper – she is waitress in the inn
3d) Sylvester Pound – he used to be an actor
4h) Homer Diesel – a *bon viveur*
5c) Jonathan Black – the mayor of Yonderwood
6i) Miles Black – the mayor's son
7g) Eleonora McDonaghough – Josy's grandmother who owns the drugstore
8a) Pastor Clark – the minister (*Pfarrer*) in the village
9e) Klara Kowalski – a strangely dressed woman

Detective Question 6:
Justus wants to scare the person who is pretending to be a vampire. *Justus hofft, dass der Schuldige vielleicht einen Fehler macht, wenn er erfährt, dass die 3 ??? ermitteln. Außerdem braucht er die Hilfe der Dorfbewohner.*

Chapter 7:
9. What's wrong?
In the morning, Mary Stamper runs out of the house screaming. Her ~~pyjamas are~~ (nightgown is) covered with blood. She collapses on the ground. ~~Pastor Clark carries~~ (The Three Investigators carry) her back to the house and ~~takes~~ (take) her pulse. The garlic and the crosses have been moved into the ~~bedroom~~ (kitchen). Justus is surprised that there is so ~~little~~ (much) blood.

Detective Question 7:
If the person who gave Mary the wound wasn't a real vampire, he could have moved the garlic and crosses himself.

Chapter 8:

10. Collecting evidence
1. To find out more, The Three Investigators **examine/search** the victims' houses.
2. They are hoping to find **clues/evidence**.
3. They are looking for anything that is **unusual/strange**.
4. In some of the houses, they **notice** that things have been moved and damaged.

Detective Question 8:
Maybe someone was looking for something.
Es handelt sich offensichtlich nicht um einen gewöhnlichen Einbruch, da zumindest auf den ersten Blick nichts entwendet wurde. Die Tatsache, dass es leichte Schäden gibt, Schlösser geknackt wurden und Dinge leicht verschoben wurden, weist darauf hin, dass jemand die Häuser gründlich durchsucht hat.

Chapter 9:

11. Information
Finde die richtige Antwort:
1c) At first Peter does not get much information from the victims because they are scared of the vampire.
2b) Otis Stamper does not leave Yonderwood because he cannot sell his house.
3b) Peter thinks Klara Kowalski is a kind of medium.
4a) Bob finds out that Yonderwood was founded by a man from Transylvania.

Detective Question 9:
silva = Wald, trans = jenseits von

Chapter 10:

12. Vampire Crossword

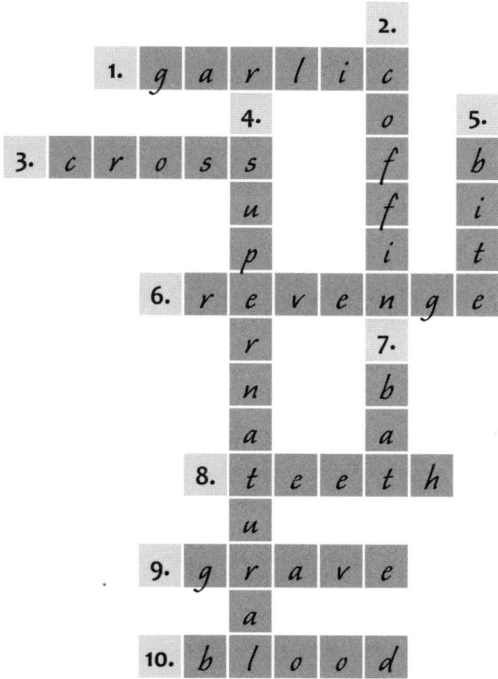

Detective Question 10:

It is strange that the vampire is in the church tower because the church is the House of God.

Als Kreaturen der Finsternis meiden Vampire normalerweise alles, was mit Religion zu tun hat. Deshalb werden auch Kruzifixe benutzt, um Vampire abzuhalten.

Chapter 11:

13. In the cemetery
1. cemetery, 2. bury, 3. coffin, 4. grave, 5. tombstone, 6. skeleton

Detective Question 11:
There is no answer to this question in the text, so you have to guess.
Vielleicht hat Zelea während seines Lebens eine Fehde mit einem der anderen Dorfbewohner gehabt und rächt sich jetzt an dessen Nachfahren. Oder vielleicht hat einer der Bewohner etwas aus seinem Grab gestohlen und Zelea rächt sich deshalb am ganzen Dorf.

Chapter 12:

14 Combine!
1b) The church tower is full of sawdust because the woodwork is being repaired.
2c) There is a hook in the wall because the workers need it to pull the wood up to the tower.
3a) The boys leave the tower quickly because the church bells are going to start ringing.
4d) The trail of sawdust is strange because it stops in front of the altar.

Detective Question 12:
It is strange that the trail of sawdust only leads in one direction (*Richtung*) and stops at the altar.
Man würde erwarten, eine Spur zu finden, die wieder vom Altar wegführt.

Chapter 13:

15 How good is your memory?
a rope *(Seil)*, a zip wire trolley *(Rollengleiter)*, pages with Bible verses *(Zettel mit Bibelversen)*, a syringe *(Kanüle)*, sleeping pills *(Schlaftabletten)*, a cape *(ein Umhang)*, an old diary *(ein altes Tagebuch)*, a medicine box, *(Schachtel mit Medikamenten)*

Detective Question 13:
The 'vampire' wasn't really flying, he was gliding down on a rope. *Der angebliche Vampir befestigte ein Seil an dem Haken des Kirchtums und an dem Ring vor dem Laden auf der Straße. Dann ließ er sich mit Hilfe eines Rollengleiters an diesem Seil vom Kirchturm bis zum Boden gleiten.*

Chapter 14:

16. Combine!
1d) take turns, 2a) hurry up, 3e) tie someone up, 4c) vanish into thin air, 5f) take a break, 6b) black eye

Verben, die im Deutschen reflexiv sind, es aber im Englischen nicht sind:

hurry up = *sich beeilen*
take turns = *sich abwechseln*

Detective Question 14:
Justus knows there is a connection because there is a draught.
Damit ein Luftzug entsteht, muss Luft sowohl herein als auch herauskommen können. Die eine Öffnung war der Eingang beim Altar, aber es musste noch eine zweite geben. Also gab es auch in der Gruft eine Verbindung zur Außenwelt.

Chapter 15:

17. Fill the gaps!
1. In the Bible verses, The Three Investigators find clues for four places: a cliff that's shaped like a dog's head, a church, the statue of a lion and a **waterfall**.
2. They look up the places on their **map**.
3. When they connect the places on the map, they find the place where the **treasure/loot** is hidden.
4. They find it in a hole in a **tree/oak tree/tree trunk**.
5. But then, a stranger comes and points a **pistol/gun** at them.
6. When Justus does not give him the bag, he **shoots** at the tree.
7. Peter gives him the bag and he **runs** away.

Detective Question 15:
They are clues for the hiding place (Versteck) of the treasure. *In jedem der Bibelverse kommt ein Ausdruck vor, der für einen markanten Punkt in Yonderwood und Umgebung steht. Verbindet man diese, so findet man den Ort, wo der Schatz versteckt ist.*

Chapter 16:

18. Bob's report
A) Ken the Cat's treasure was hidden in a tree. After he died, the people in the village found the gold. Because they could not find out who the reall (real) owner was, they decided to put it in a safe place. The Bibel (Bible) verses were clues for the hiding place. Somebody found out about the treasure when he found an old diery (diary). He pretended to be a vampire so that he could search the victims' houses. The blood on the pillows was animal blood.

Detective Question 16:
They want to find out something about the way people kick and catch. *Am wahrscheinlichsten ist es, dass sie herausfinden wollen, mit welchem Fuß die Dorfbewohner treten und mit welcher Hand sie fangen. Vielleicht ist ihnen aber auch etwas an der Art, wie sich der Mann mit Pistole bewegt hat, aufgefallen, und sie wollen nun sehen, ob sie es bei einem der Dorfbewohner beobachten können.*

Chapter 17:

19. What happens when?
Reihenfolge der Sätze: b, d, a, e, g, c, f

Detective Question 17:
Jonathan Black was one of the victims because that was the easiest way for Miles to start the spook. *Zwar brauchte Miles von seinem Vater keine Informationen, da er das Tagebuch von Xavier Noir schon bei den Renovierungsarbeiten entdeckt hatte. Trotzdem bot es sich an, einen Vampirbesuch vorzutäuschen, da er in seinem eigenen Haus leicht Zugang zum Zimmer seines Vaters hatte.*

Die drei ??? ... ihre großen Fälle!

- ☐ Angriff der Computerviren
  978-3-440-11674-6
- ☐ Fußball-Gangster
  978-3-440-11675-3
- ☐ Vampir im Internet
  978-3-440-11676-0
- ☐ Insektenstachel
  978-3-440-11677-7
- ☐ Tal des Schreckens
  978-3-440-11678-4
- ☐ Hexenhandy
  978-3-440-11679-1
- ☐ Gift per E-Mail
  978-3-440-11680-7
- ☐ und der Schatz der Mönche
  978-3-440-11681-4
- ☐ Die sieben Tore
  978-3-440-11682-1
- ☐ Das Auge des Drachen
  978-3-440-11683-8
- ☐ Villa der Toten
  978-3-440-11684-5
- ☐ Auf tödlichem Kurs
  978-3-440-11685-2
- ☐ Der finstere Rivale
  978-3-440-11686-9
- ☐ Das düstere Vermächtnis
  978-3-440-11687-6
- ☐ Der schwarze Skorpion
  978-3-440-11688-3
- ☐ und der Geisterzug
  978-3-440-11692-0
- ☐ Spur ins Nichts
  978-3-440-11693-7
- ☐ Fußballfieber
  978-3-440-11691-3
- ☐ Schrecken aus dem Moor
  978-3-440-11689-0
- ☐ Geister-Canyon
  978-3-440-11690-6
- ☐ SMS aus dem Grab
  978-3-440-11695-1
- ☐ Schatten über Hollywood
  978-3-440-11696-8
- ☐ Schwarze Madonna
  978-3-440-11694-4
- ☐ Fluch des Drachen
  978-3-440-11698-2
- ☐ Spuk im Netz
  978-3-440-11697-5
- ☐ Haus des Schreckens
  978-3-440-11699-9
- ☐ Fluch des Piraten
  978-3-440-11701-9
- ☐ Fels der Dämonen
  978-3-440-11700-2
- ☐ Der tote Mönch
  978-3-440-11703-3
- ☐ und das versunkene Dorf
  978-3-440-11705-7
- ☐ Pfad der Angst
  978-3-440-11702-6
- ☐ Die geheime Treppe
  978-3-440-11704-0
- ☐ Das Geheimnis der Diva
  978-3-440-11708-8
- ☐ und die Fußball-Falle
  978-3-440-11706-4
- ☐ Stadt der Vampire
  978-3-440-11707-1
- ☐ Zwillinge der Finsternis
  978-3-440-11548-0
- ☐ und die Poker-Hölle
  978-3-440-11567-1
- ☐ Tödliches Eis
  978-3-440-11568-8
- ☐ Grusel auf Campbell Castle
  978-3-440-11920-4
- ☐ Die Rache der Samurai
  978-3-440-11906-8
- ☐ Der Biss der Bestie
  978-3-440-11919-8
- ☐ Das Gespensterschloss
  978-3-440-11921-3
- ☐ Schwarze Sonne
  978-3-440-11875-7
- ☐ und die feurige Flut
  978-3-440-11876-4

☐ Der namenlose Gegner
978-3-440-11877-1

www.kosmos.de/die_drei_fragezeichen

Jeder Band mit 128 Seiten
Je €/D 7,95
Preisänderung vorbehalten